Key Stage 3

Maths

Ages 11-12

Sheila Hunt

survival GUIDE

Letts Educational
Chiswick Centre
414 Chiswick High Road
London W4 5TF
Tel: 020 8996 3333
Fax: 020 8996 8390
Email: mail@lettsed.co.uk
Website: www.letts-education.com

First published 2001

10 9 8 7 6 5 4 3

British Library Cataloging in Publication Data. A CIP record of this book is available from the British Library.

ISBN 1 84085 636 X

Letts Educational Limited is a division of Granada Learning Limited, part of Granada plc.

Edited and typeset by Cambridge Publishing Management.

Designed by Moondisks Limited

Maths

Book 1 Ages 11–12

Introduction

Do you recognise yourself?
You are:
- about to start at secondary school and wondering if you'll be able to cope in maths
- already at secondary school, and having a few problems in maths
- supposed to be revising for a test or exam in maths, but don't know where to start
- usually all right in maths, but there's just a few topics where you come unstuck
- a parent or helper at your wits end trying to lend a hand with homework.

If any of this sounds familiar, then this book could be just what you are looking for. *Letts Key Stage 3 Maths Survival Guide Ages 11–12* will take you through all the topics which you are likely to find in the first secondary school year (Year 7). You can work through it from beginning to end, or use it as a handy source of reference to check up on a troublesome topic, or any topics that are missed. There are explanations and worked examples to help to help iron out any problems, and short exercises, all with answers, for you to practise your growing skills. Notice too the 'Tactics', giving you handy hints and tips, and the 'Red alerts', which warn you to take extra care to avoid those common mistakes which most of us make from time to time.

Setting out on your secondary school career can seem daunting and so we have included a few 'Survival sheets' to make this exciting time in your life as easy and enjoyable as possible.

The number network
Just to reassure you – this map on page 5 is for reference only, you are not expected to learn it! The number network is a quick way to check up on the skills you need before you tackle a new topic or process. You can't, for example, solve probability questions without knowing about fractions, decimals or percentages. The number network shows you which areas you need to know before you tackle something unfamiliar, and also just how far that newly-acquired skill could take you.

Have a good trip!

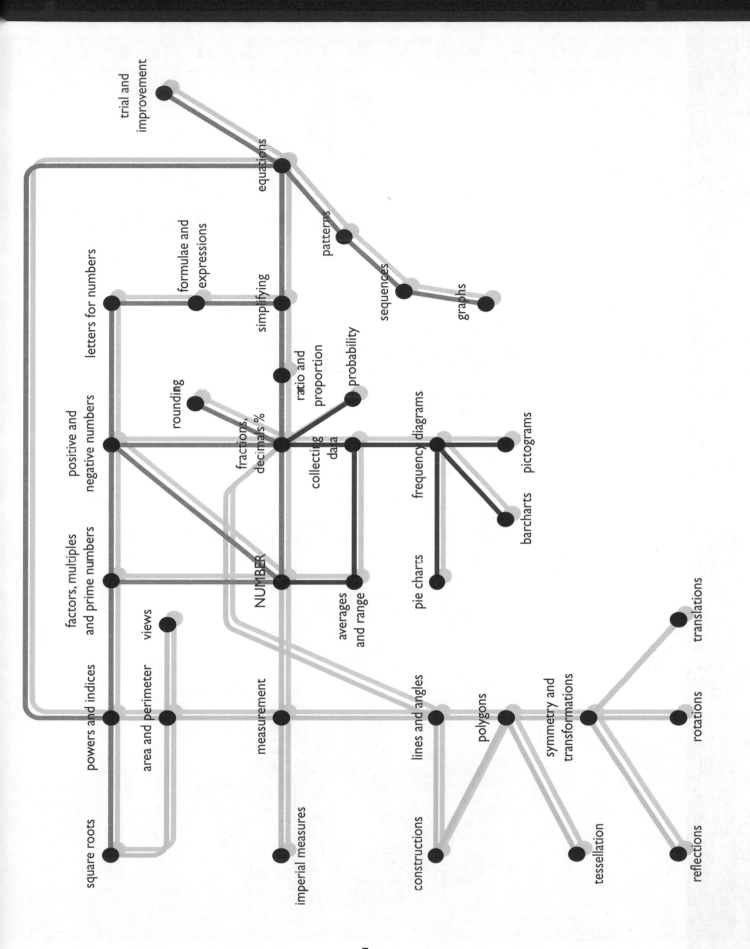

1

All change! Starting Year 7

Becoming a Year 7 student brings lots of changes:
- getting used to a new and bigger school building
- meeting different teachers for every subject
- having more homework and tests
- taking more responsibility for yourself.

However, you will also find:
- new friends
- new subjects
- new interests
- new opportunities and a fresh start.

To ease your way into secondary school life, and to help you get the best out of this big change to your life, it pays to *get organised*.
Even if you are already a Year 7 student, you may find some new ideas here that are worth trying.

Things to do: sort out somewhere to work

- Find a space where you can keep all your school books, folders and the other general clutter that you will soon accumulate. Having a special shelf for books is useful and makes them easy to find. You can also use baskets, large plastic crates or even sturdy cardboard boxes for storage, and perhaps you could keep these all together, under the bed or at the bottom of a wardrobe.

- If you have several containers, it's a good idea to label them clearly, or to use different colours for different subjects.

- It's much easier to keep track of everything if you have several small containers rather than one huge one. Inside a large box, you can have smaller, labelled boxes.

- Plastic trays are also useful as you can keep unfinished projects in them. When you need to use the material, you can easily carry it to wherever you are planning to work, and you are less likely to lose that essential sheet that took you so long to write. You can often see cheap plastic trays in bargain shops, markets or even pet shops! They are also available in a wide range of colours to help your filing system.

- If you have some wall space, a notice board can be useful. You can then pin up helpful reminders to yourself such as, 'PE tomorrow. Remember kit.'

- Try pinning up a copy of your school timetable. Your school may operate a two-week or six- or seven-day cycle. You will be surprised how soon you get used to it, but it can be confusing when you start.

The number system

Understanding the jargon

Integer whole number
Digit individual numeral in a number: 6 has one digit, 20 has two digits, as does 3.4.

Place value

Using just the ten symbols 0, 1, 2, 3, 4, 5, 6, 7, 8, 9 in the decimal number system, you can write any number, no matter how big or small it is, as long as you write each digit in the correct position. This is its place value.

Understanding place value

The decimal number system uses 'bundles' of ten individual values.
When you have ten units (the next number after 9), you have 1 bundle of ten and 0 left over. That is why ten is written as 10.
The next number after 99 gives 10 bundles of ten. This needs a new bundle, called hundreds: 100. After hundreds come thousands, then tens of thousands and hundreds of thousands, and so on. Still thinking of each of these as a bundle, each has its own position in the place-value system.
Notice that every group of three bundles breaks down into hundreds, tens, units (HTU).
You need to write a digit in each of the HTU spaces, to show, for instance, the difference between ten thousand and just plain ten.

	Thousands			Units		
Hundreds of thousands	Tens of thousands	Thousands	Hundreds	Tens	Units	
				1	0	ten
	1	0	0	0	0	ten thousand
1	0	0	0	0	0	one hundred thousand

The next group is millions, tens of millions and hundreds of millions, then all the billions and tens of billions and hundreds of billions, then all the trillions… and so on for ever and ever and ever…

Exercise 1

Write each of the following numbers in figures.
The first one has been done for you.

1 two thousand, three hundred and one

If you read this out to yourself you can hear that it has two thousands bundles, three hundreds bundles, no tens and one unit.
You can then fill in a table like this.
So the answer is 2301.

Thousands	Hundreds	Tens	Units
2	3	0	1

2 thirty thousand and eighteen

3 two million, one hundred and five thousand and nine

How to write numbers up to 9999

Writing numbers up to and including nine thousand, nine hundred and ninety-nine is easy. Just write one digit in each column, without separating them by commas or spaces.

Remember to write zero in any blank columns. You *do* need to use commas to write numbers in words, though.

Example
2356	two thousand, three hundred and fifty-six
2350	two thousand, three hundred and fifty
2305	two thousand, three hundred and five
2007	two thousand and seven

How to write numbers greater than 999

Example
Write one hundred and twenty-six thousand, three hundred and eighty-four in figures.

Split the number into groups.
Write 126 in the thousands group.

Millions	Thousands	Units
HTU	HTU	HTU
	126	

Then fill in the hundreds, tens and units group.

Millions	Thousands	Units	
HTU	HTU	HTU	
	126	384	= 126 384

Example
Write the number one million, seventy thousand and one in figures.

Millions	Thousands	Units	
one	seventy	one	
HTU	HTU	HTU	
1	070	001	= 1 070 001

Remember, you must have one digit in every place-value column to the right of the first digit.

How to read very large numbers

Sometimes you will see very large numbers with no spaces to help you work out what they are. Many calculators, for instance, will display numbers with up to ten digits.

Example
Write the number 4 832 180 in words.
Try writing headings over the digits.

M	Hth	Tth	Th	H	T	U
4	8	3	2	1	8	0

Then separate the number into groups of three digits, starting from the right. 4 832 180
The number is four million, eight hundred and thirty-two thousand, one hundred and eighty.

Exercise 2

Write each of these numbers in words.
1 4 600 034
2 2 019 003
3 6 004 080

Tactics
You must have a digit in every column to the right of the first number.

9

How to multiply or divide integers by a power of 10

Understanding the jargon

Integer whole number
Power of 10 10, 100, 1000, ...

How to multiply

Example

H	T	U			M	Hth	Tth	Th	H	T	U
		3 × 10	=							3	0
	3	2 × 10	=						3	2	0
		3 × 100	=						3	0	0
	3	2 × 100	=					3	2	0	0
		3 × 1000	=					3	0	0	0
	3	2 × 1000	=				3	2	0	0	0

3 × 10	=	30	3 × 100	=	300

3 × 1000 = 3000
32 × 10 = 320   32 × 100 = 3200   32 × 1000 = 32 000

Multiplying an integer by ten moves each digit in the integer one place to the left.
Multiplying an integer by a hundred moves each digit in the integer two places to the left.
Multiplying an integer by a thousand moves each digit in the integer three places to the left.
Put a zero in the space that appears every time the digits move one place to the left.

How to multiply an integer by a multiple of 10 (20, 30, ...)

Example
37 × 20
Write the zero at the right-hand end of the answer first.
This will move all the digits one place to the left, taking care of the ×10 part.
But 20 = 10 × 2, so you need to work out 37 × 10 × 2.
37 × 20 = 370 × 2 = 740

Exercise 3

1 a 750 × 100   b 560 × 100
   c 2300 × 1000
2 a 3400 ÷ 10   b 1 000 000 ÷ 100

Exercise 4

1 48 × 40
2 36 × 80
3 46 × 20
4 17 × 60
5 29 × 70

How to divide

$$30 \div 10 = 3 \qquad 300 \div 100 = 3 \qquad 3000 \div 1000 = 3$$
$$320 \div 10 = 32 \qquad 3200 \div 100 = 32 \qquad 32\,000 \div 1000 = 32$$

Multiplying and dividing are inverse operations.

Dividing an integer by ten moves each digit in the integer one place to the right.

Dividing an integer by a hundred moves each digit in the integer two **places** to the right.

Dividing an integer by a thousand moves each digit in the integer three places to the right.

Fitting decimals into the number system

How to read and write numbers with decimals

$$1\,000\,000 \div 10 = 100\,000$$
$$100\,000 \div 10 = 10\,000$$
$$10\,000 \div 10 = 1000$$
$$1000 \div 10 = 100$$
$$100 \div 10 = 10$$
$$10 \div 10 = 1$$
$$1.0 \div 10 = 0.1 \text{ or one tenth}$$
$$0.1 \div 10 = 0.01 \text{ or one hundredth}$$
$$0.01 \div 10 = 0.001 \text{ or one thousandth} \ldots \text{and so on}$$

The decimal point separates the integers (whole numbers) from the parts of the number that are less than one whole (the decimal fractions).

In decimal numbers, the largest digit allowed in any column is 9. Adding into this column affects the digit in the next column to the left.

Example
Add 0.01 to 0.09
This gives the next number as 0.1.

Example
Add 0.1 to 0.9
This gives 1 whole unit.

Usually, but not always, you can omit zeros at the end of a decimal fraction. $1.5 = 1.50$

Exercise 5

Do not use a calculator for this exercise.

1   Use each digit once in each answer: 7 2 9 3
   a   Make the smallest odd number you can.   b   Make the largest number you can.
2   Add: a $0.009 + 0.001$ b $0.09 + 0.1$ c $0.01 + 0.009$
3   Start with 34286. Keep the digits in the same order.
   a   Write the number as an integer, spacing correctly.
   b   Write the number in words.
   c   Insert a decimal point so that:
      i   the 3 is worth three hundred
      ii   the 2 is worth two hundredths.

Tactics

When reading a decimal number aloud, say each digit of the decimal fraction part individually. For example, 3.24 is read as 'three point two four', *not* 'three point twenty-four'.

RT RED ALERT RED ALERT! R   T

Using decimals

Decimal places

The number of digits after the decimal point is the number of decimal places.
0.31 has been written correct to two decimal places (2 d.p.).
23.147 has been written correct to 3 d.p.
2.0003 has been written correct to 4 d.p.
The unit on Rounding and estimating (page 18) will explain more about decimal places.

Decimal numbers

The closer a decimal digit is to the decimal point, the higher its value.
The 1 in 3.1 is worth more than the 9 in 3.09, even though 9 is bigger than 1.
This is easier to understand if you think about money.
£3.10 is worth more than £3.09.

How to multiply a number containing a decimal by a power of 10
With each multiplication, every digit moves one place to the left, jumping over the point if necessary.

Example

H	T	U	.	tenths	hundredths	thousandths			Th	H	T	U	.	tenths	hundredths	thousandths
		2	.	6	5		4 × 10	=			2	6	.	5	4	
		2	.	6	5		4 × 100	=		2	6	5	.	4		
		2	.	6	5		4 × 1000	=	2	6	5	4				

2.654 ×   10 =   26.54
2.654 ×   100 =   265.4
2.654 × 1000 = 2654

Exercise 1

1   Write the larger of each pair of numbers.
   a   2.325 or 2.523   **b**   17.24 or 17.168   **c**   0.99 or 1.001
2   Put these numbers in order, from smallest to largest.
   a   0.3, 0.14, 0.031, 0.002. 1.006   **b**   3.01, 1.95, 0.34, 0.002

Exercise 2

Work these out without using a calculator.
1   43.2 × 60   2   23.5 × 30   3   2.46 × 20   4   3.08 × 40   5   0.03 × 20

How to multiply a number containing a decimal by a multiple of 10

Example
5.3 × 40
5.3 × 10 = 53
53 × 4 = 212
5.3 × 40 = 212

Example
2.17 × 30
2.17 × 10 = 21.7
21.7 × 3 = 65.1
2.17 × 30 = 65.1

Example
34.23 × 20
34.23 × 10 = 342.3
342.3 × 2 = 684.6
34.23 × 20 = 684.6

Example
0.134 × 60
0.134 × 10 = 1.34
1.34 × 6 = 8.04
0.134 × 60 = 8.04

How to multiply a decimal number by any two-digit number

Example
3.24 × 23
3.24 × 20 = 64.8 (3.24 × 10 × 2)
3.24 × 3 = 9.72
3.24 × 23 = 64.8 + 9.72 = 74.52
Another way of setting out your work is like this.

```
    3.24                              3.24
  × 23                              × 23
   64.8      3.24 × 20     or        9.72      3.24 × 3
   9.72      3.24 × 3               64.8       3.24 × 20
  74.52                             74.52
```

How to multiply an integer by 0.1, 0.01, ...

Multiplying a number by 0.1 is the same as multiplying it by one tenth or finding a tenth of it. Finding a tenth of a number is the same as dividing by ten.

Example
32 × 0.1 = 32 ÷ 10 = 3.2

Multiplying a number by 0.01 is the same as multiplying by one hundredth, or finding a hundredth of it. To find a hundredth, divide by 100.

Example
32 × 0.01 = 32 ÷ 100 = 0.32

Exercise 3

1 29.3 × 15 2 34.1 × 56 3 43.5 × 24
4 23.4 × 15 5 1.17 × 26

Exercise 4

1 45 × 0.1 2 45 × 0.01 3 150 × 0.1
4 150 × 0.01 5 24 × 0.1 = 24 ÷ ?

Note that the 1 is still worth 1 unit and the 7 is still worth 7 tenths, whether you write 1.7, 1.70, 1.700, 1.7000, ... Their values will only change if you change their positions to 0.017, 0.17, 17, 170, ... **RED ALERT**

Types of number

Understanding the jargon

Factor a number that divides into another number without leaving a remainder

Multiple a number that can be divided by a factor

Product the result of multiplying two or more numbers together

Sum the result of adding two or more numbers together

Prime number a number that has two and only two factors – itself and one

Prime factor a factor that is also a prime number

Square number the result of multiplying a number by itself

Square root the number that is multiplied by itself to give a square number

Examples

- $12 \div 3 = 4$ so 3 is a factor of 12.
  $10 \div 2 = 5$ so 2 is a factor of 10.
- $2 \times 5 = 10$ so 10 is a multiple of 5.
  $3 \times 7 = 21$ so 21 is a multiple of 7.
- $5 \times 2 = 10$ so the product of 5 and 2 is 10.
- $5 + 2 = 7$. The sum of 5 and 2 is 7.
- 17 is a prime number, because its only factors are 1 and 17.
  23 is a prime number because its only factors are 1 and 23.
- Factors of 12 are 1, 2, 3, 4, 6 and 12.
  2 and 3 are prime numbers, so 2 and 3 are prime factors of 12.
  1, 4, 6 and 12 are not prime numbers so they are not prime factors of 12.
- 25 is a square number because $5 \times 5 = 25$. You can write 25 as 5^2, read as 'five squared'.
  1 is a square number, because $1 \times 1 = 1$ or $1^2 = 1$.
- $5 \times 5 = 25$, so the square root of 25 is 5. It is written $\sqrt{25} = 5$.

Exercise 1

1 Write down two factors of each number.
   a 8   b 12   c 13   d 19
2 Write down the first four multiples of each number.
   a 4   b 5   c 6   d 9
3 Which of these numbers are primes?
   1 2 3 4 5 6 7 8 9 10 11 12

Exercise 2

1 List the prime factors of:
   a 15   b 30   c 144
2 What is five to the power of three?
3 What is the square root of thirty-six?

RED ALERT!   1 is not a prime number, as it has only one factor – itself.
2^5 is not 2×5 but $2 \times 2 \times 2 \times 2 \times 2$!   RED

Powers or indices

A number multiplied by itself gives a square number. Multiplied by itself again it gives a cube number. You can go on multiplying a number by itself. This is called raising a number to a power.

$2 \times 2 \times 2 \times 2 \times 2 = 2^5 = 32$

2 is the base. 5 is the index (plural indices). 32 is 'two raised to the power of five'.

Examples

$2^4 = 2 \times 2 \times 2 \times 2 = 16$ Two to the power of four is sixteen.

$3^4 = 3 \times 3 \times 3 \times 3 = 81$ Three to the power of four is eighty-one

---

How to write a number as a product of prime factors

Examples

Write 240 as a product of prime factors. There are several different ways of doing this. One way is to use a factor tree. Split 240 into a pair of factors with product 240. Now continue to split each pair in the same way.

There can be more than one way of developing the factor tree, but whichever way you choose, you should finish with the same numbers at the bottom. Remember that 1 itself is not a prime number, so no line should end with 1.

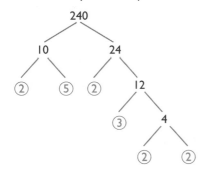

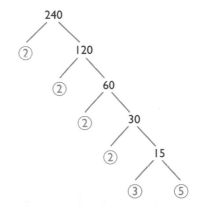

The prime numbers are at the end of the line, so put a ring round each prime number. When every line ends with a ringed prime number, you cannot go any further.

$240 = 2 \times 2 \times 2 \times 2 \times 3 \times 5$. This is usually written with indices. $240 = 2^4 \times 3 \times 5$

Exercise 3

1 Write each of the following numbers as a product of prime factors.
   a   288
   b   250

2 These numbers have been written as the product of prime factors.
   What are the numbers?
   a $2^3 \times 3^2 \times 7$
   b $3^3 \times 5^2$

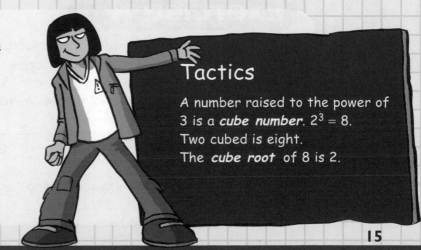

Tactics

A number raised to the power of 3 is a *cube number*. $2^3 = 8$. Two cubed is eight. The *cube root* of 8 is 2.

RT RED ALERT RED ALERT! RED ALERT RED ALERT

Positive and negative numbers

All numbers have a place somewhere on a never-ending number line.

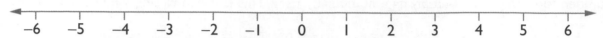

A number that has a value of less than zero is a negative number.
Negative numbers appear to the left of zero on the number line.
Read −3 as 'negative 3', read −1.5 as 'negative 1.5'.

In the real world, for instance on a weather forecast, you may hear negative numbers referred to as 'minus numbers'. The forecaster may say, 'The temperature tonight will be minus eight.'

Example
(−3) + 5
Using the number line above, put your pencil on −3. Move it forward 5 places and it should finish on 2.
(−3) + 5 = 2

Example
7 + (−2)
Put your pencil on 7. Move it back 2 places and it should finish on 5.
7 + (−2) = 5

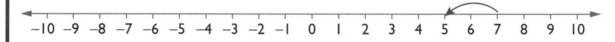

Exercise 4

1 Put these numbers in order of size, starting with the smallest. 2, −6, −8, 5, 3, 1
2 Write the larger of each pair of integers.
   a 2 or −8   **b** −3 or −10   **c** −5 or 1
3 Count backwards in twos along this number line, from 7 to −9. The first jump is shown.

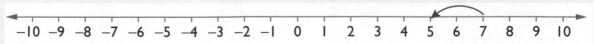

4 Using the number line again, start another pattern starting at −9 and add on three each time, −9, −6, ...
5 Which integers are in both patterns?

Remember, whenever two negative signs meet head on, like this – –, it can make them cross.

Take care when you add or subtract negative numbers. These examples may help.

$10 + (-1)$

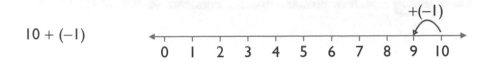

$(-5) + (-3)$

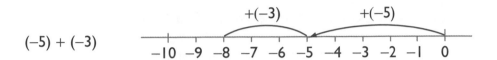

Example

Imagine that you have ten sweets and that you offer one to your friend.
That would leave you with $10 + (-1) = 10 - 1 = 9$ sweets.
However, your friend does not want it, and gives it back.
You have $9 - (-1) = 9 + 1 = 10$.

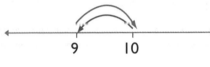

Examples

You buy a present for your best friend for £5.00 and lose £3.00 on the way home from the shops. How much less money have you now? $(-5) + (-3) = (-8)$

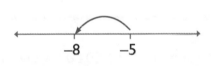

Exercise 5

Work these out. You can use a number line to help you.

1 $(-2) + 7$ **2** $3 + (-5)$ **3** $(-4) + (-6)$
4 $5 - (-3)$ **5** $(-2) + (-5)$ **6** $(-1) - (-3)$

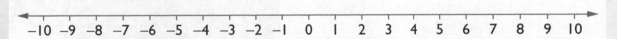

17

Rounding and estimating

How to round numbers using decimal places (d.p.)

Rounding means writing a number with fewer non-zero digits than it started with.
The result is less exact, but it may be more useful, for example, if you are working with an amount of money.
To round a number, first underline the digit immediately after the one you need. If the value is 5 or more, you usually round up; if it is 4 or less, you usually round down.

> **Example**
> Write 4.784 71 correct to 2 d.p.
> The question asks for 2 d.p., so underline the third digit after the point.
> 4.784 71
> The value is less than 5, so round down.
> 4.784 71 = 4.78 to 2 d.p.

> **Example**
> Write 4.784 71 correct to 3 d.p.
> The question asks for 3 d.p., so underline the fourth digit after the point.
> 4.784 71
> The value is greater than 5, so round up.
> 4.784 71 = 4.785 to 3 d.p.

> **Example**
> Write 4.75 correct to 1 d.p.
> When the underlined digit is 5, round up
> 4.75 = 4.8 to 1 d.p.

> **Example**
> Write 3.498 correct to 2 d.p.
> Round up, as 8 is larger than 4. 49 rounds to 50, so the answer is 3.498 = 3.50 to 2 d.p.

How to use rounding in practical situations

> **Example**
> Gemma needs to save £60.00 for Christmas presents. She thinks she can save between £3.80 and £4.25 each week. She aims to do all her shopping in the first week of December. When should she start to save? Gemma saves roughly £4.00 a week.
> 60.00 ÷ 4 = 15 so it will take her 15 weeks to save £60.
> It will take her about four months to save enough money, so she should start saving at the beginning of August.

Exercise 1

1. Write these numbers correct to two decimal places.
   a 23.463 **b** 16.077 **c** 8.698
2. Write these numbers correct to one decimal place.
   a 6.07 **b** 34.97 **c** 23.06
3. Give these amounts to the nearest penny.
   a £23.145 **b** £0.671 **c** £7.58 × 10
   d £1.06 × 10 **e** £34.20 ÷ 10 **f** £0.20 × 10
   g £10.45 ÷ 10 **h** £15.00 ÷ 100
4. **a** Write 462p in pounds
   b Write £3.04 in pence.

> **Tactics**
>
> You may sometimes be asked to give an answer to the nearest penny. This is really the same as giving an answer to two decimal places.

If you are asked to round a number to 2 d.p. you must have two digits after the decimal point. Use common sense when it comes to rounding up or down.

ALERT RED

How to estimate

Sometimes you don't need a very accurate answer – a good estimate is close enough. Also, it is wise to work out a rough answer or estimate before tackling a maths problem so that you will know whether your final answer is sensible.

> ### Example
> Find a rough answer for 19.3×36.1.
> We can round this calculation to 20×36. $20 \times 36 = 720$
> $19.3 \times 36.1 = 696.73$
>
> The rounded answer is close enough to the actual answer to be a sensible estimate. If you used a calculator but pressed the decimal point key in the wrong place to get the answer 69.673, working out an estimate should immediately alert you to the fact that something is wrong somewhere!

How to find a midpoint

The midpoint (halfway mark) between 6 and 10 is 8.
The midpoint between 6 and 8 is 7.

The midpoint between 6 and 7 is 6.5.

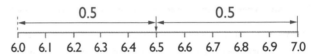

The midpoint between 6.4 and 6.5 is 6.45.

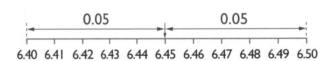

To find the midpoint between two numbers:

* find the difference between the two numbers
* divide the difference by two
* add this difference to the smaller number, or subtract it from the larger number.

Exercise 2

Do not use a calculator. Estimate the answers.
1 59.1×3.7 2 24.89×4.1 3 $510 \div 11$ 4 £82.96 – £19.79
5 £148.99 + £202. 13

Exercise 3

Find the midpoint between the numbers in each of these pairs.
1 12 and 18   2 13 and 16   3 10.6 and 10.7   4 5.3 and 5.4

RT If you need 5.1 coaches for a school trip, you will have to book 6 coaches, or leave some students behind. If your calculation tells you that you can fit 10.9 boxes of china into a crate, you can only pack 10 boxes without risking breakages.

Decimals, percentages and fractions

Understanding the jargon

Per cent (%) means per hundred.
58% means 58 per 100 or 58 out of 100. It is also the same as 58 hundredths or 0.58.
The whole amount is 100%.
If 75% of a group of students pass an examination, then 25% fail.
If 87% of the members of a youth club own bikes, then 13% do not own bikes.

Percentages and decimals

To turn a decimal into a percentage, first write the decimal correct to two decimal places.

> **Example**
> 15p = 15 hundredths of a pound = £0.15
> 0.15 = 15%

> **Example**
> 0.368 = 0.37 to 2 d.p. = 37%
> 0.4 = 0.40 = 40%

How to find a percentage of a number

> **Example**
> Find 10 per cent of 65.
> 10% = 0.1
> $65 \times 0.1 = 6.5$ (or $65 \div 10 = 6.5$)

> **Example**
> Find 1% of 48.
> 1% = 0.01
> $48 \times 0.01 = 0.48$ (or $48 \div 100 = 0.48$)

Multiplying by 0.1 is the same as dividing by 10. Multiplying by 0.01 is the same as dividing by 100.

> **Remember!**
> 1% = 0.01 Divide the quantity by 100.
> 10% = 0.1 Divide the quantity by 10.
> 50% = 0.5 Divide the quantity by 2.

> **Example**
> Find 4% of 240.
> 1% = 2.4
> $4\% = 2.4 \times 4 = 9.6$

Exercise 1

1 Change the following decimals into percentages.
   a 0.45   b 0.72   c 0.07   d 0.461   e 0.578   f 0.066
2 Change the following percentages into decimals.
   a 43%   b 28%   c 25%   d 6%   e 9%   f 5%

Exercise 2

Do not use a calculator to work these out.
1 10% of 54   2 7% of 80. (**Hint**: Start by finding 1%.)
3 50% of 70   4 20% of 60 (**Hint**: Start by finding 10%.)

In books, you may see fractions written in different ways. For instance, $\frac{2}{3}$ is the same as 2/3.   RED

Fractions

Understanding the jargon

Fraction When you divide something into equal parts, the results are fractions.
Each part of a cake divided equally into ten is $1 \div 10$ or $\frac{1}{10}$
Two cakes shared equally among three people is $2 \div 3$ or $\frac{2}{3}$
Denominator The number at the bottom of a fraction is the denominator. It tells you how many equal parts there are in the whole. It shows you the fraction family that the fraction belongs to. The fraction three-quarters has a denominator of four. It belongs to the family of quarters.
Numerator The number at the top of a fraction is the numerator. It tells you how many fractional parts there are in the fraction. The fraction three-quarters has a numerator of three. You have three fractional parts.

Improper fractions

A fraction with the numerator greater than the denominator is an improper fraction.
$\frac{13}{5}$ is an improper fraction. Improper fractions are also called top-heavy fractions.

Mixed numbers

A number made up of an integer and a fraction is a mixed number. $3\frac{2}{5}$ is a mixed number.

Equivalent fractions

Two or more fractions that have the same value are equivalent fractions.
One half ($\frac{1}{2}$) and two quarters ($\frac{2}{4}$) are equivalent fractions.
To make two equivalent fractions, multiply or divide the numerator and the denominator by the same number.

$$\frac{2}{5} \xrightarrow{\times 2} = \xrightarrow{\times 2} \frac{4}{10} \qquad \frac{12}{15} \xrightarrow{\div 3} = \xrightarrow{\div 3} \frac{4}{5}$$

Exercise 3

Complete the following equivalent fractions.

1 $\frac{3}{4} = \frac{6}{8} = \frac{12}{?}$

2 $\frac{3}{5} = \frac{9}{?} = \frac{?}{45}$

3 $\frac{2}{3} = \frac{?}{6} = \frac{16}{?}$

4 $\frac{20}{50} = \frac{2}{?}$

5 $\frac{24}{40} = \frac{?}{20} = \frac{6}{?} = \frac{?}{5}$

Tactics

There is the same amount of cake in one half as in two-quarters of the same cake, so one half and two quarters are equivalent.

21

How to cancel or reduce a fraction to its simplest form

Divide the numerator and denominator by the same number until their only common factor is 1.

If you spot that the largest number which will divide into 16 and 40 is 8, you can divide by 8 straight away and reach the right answer more quickly.

> ### Example
> $\frac{16}{40} = \frac{8}{20} = \frac{4}{10} = \frac{2}{5}$

How to spot if a number will cancel

Remember, always divide the numerator and the denominator by the same number.

- All even numbers can be divided by 2.
- All numbers ending in 0 can be divided by 10.
- All numbers ending in 5 or 0 can be divided by 5.
- Numbers in which the digits add up to a number in the 3 times table can be divided by 3.
- All even numbers that can be divided by 3 can also be divided by 6.
- Numbers in which the digits add up to a number in the 9 times table can be divided by 9.

You will find it helpful if you can remember all of these points.

> ### Examples
> Which of these numbers can be divided by 3, 6 or 9 without leaving a remainder?
> 561   744   558
>
> 561:   5 + 6 + 1 = 12   12 can be divided exactly by 3.
>   561 ÷ 3 = 187
>   561 is odd so it cannot be divided exactly by 6.
>   12 cannot be divided exactly by 9, and neither can 561 (561 ÷ 9 = 62.333 333...).
>
> 744:   7 + 4 + 4 = 15   15 can be divided exactly by 3.
>   744 ÷ 3 = 248
>   744 is even so it can be divided exactly by 6.
>   744 ÷ 6 = 124
>   15 cannot be divided exactly by 9, and neither can 744 (744 ÷ 9 = 82.666...).
>
> 558:   5 + 5 + 8 = 18   18 can be divided exactly by 3.
>   558 ÷ 3 = 186
>   558 is even so it can be divided exactly by 6.
>   558 ÷ 6 = 93
>   18 can be divided exactly by 9 and so can 558.
>   558 ÷ 9 = 62.

Exercise 4

1 Which of the following numbers cannot be divided exactly by 5?
   160   72   35   80   11

2 Which of the following numbers cannot be divided exactly by 3?
   467   310   561   973   189

3 Which of the following numbers cannot be divided exactly by 9?
   534   765   411   720   942

Exercise 5

1 Give each of these fractions in its simplest form.

   a $\frac{20}{30}$ **b** $\frac{15}{25}$ **c** $\frac{6}{8}$ **d** $\frac{28}{35}$ **e** $\frac{8}{20}$

2 Which of these fractions is not equivalent to $\frac{3}{4}$?

   $\frac{30}{40}$ $\frac{75}{100}$ $\frac{6}{9}$ $\frac{12}{16}$

How to change improper fractions to mixed numbers

Example

Change $\frac{27}{4}$ to a mixed number.

$\frac{27}{4} = 27 \div 4 = 6$ remainder 3

But the remainder is really **three-quarters**, so the correct answer is $\frac{27}{4} = 6\frac{3}{4}$

Example

Change $\frac{22}{4}$ to a mixed number.

$\frac{22}{4} = 22 \div 4 = 5$ remainder 2.,

So $\frac{22}{4} = 5\frac{2}{4}$

But $\frac{2}{4} = \frac{1}{2}$ so $\frac{22}{4} = 5\frac{1}{2}$.

How to change mixed numbers to improper fractions

Examples

Change $3\frac{1}{2}$ to an improper fraction.
The denominator tells you which fraction family to use. Change the whole number into halves.
1 whole = 2 halves
so 3 wholes = 3 × 2 = 6 halves
You also have an extra half, so altogether there are 3 × 2 + 1 = 7 halves.
$3\frac{1}{2} = \frac{7}{2}$

Examples

Change $5\frac{3}{4}$ to an improper fraction.
The denominator tells you which fraction family to use. Change the whole numbers into quarters.
1 whole = 4 quarters
so 5 wholes = 5 × 4 quarters
You also have an extra three-quarters so altogether there are
5 × 4 + 3 = 23 quarters.
$5\frac{3}{4} = \frac{23}{4}$

How to find a fraction of a quantity when the numerator is 1
You already know that to find half of a number or quantity, you divide by 2.
So $\frac{1}{2}$ of £80.00 = £80.00 ÷ 2 = £40.00
To find a quarter of a number or quantity, divide by 4.
$\frac{1}{4}$ of £80.00 = £80.00 ÷ 4 = £20.00
You could halve the original amount and then halve again, but it's quicker to divide by 4.
To find a fifth, divide by 5, and so on.

Exercise 6

Change these improper fractions to mixed numbers, remembering to cancel if necessary.

1 $\frac{12}{5}$ 2 $\frac{19}{2}$ 3 $\frac{18}{4}$ 4 $\frac{26}{3}$ 5 $\frac{20}{8}$

Tactics

In a fraction, the numerator is on the top, and the denominator is on the bottom.

Exercise 7

Change these mixed numbers to improper fractions.

1 $5\frac{1}{2}$ 2 $2\frac{3}{4}$ 3 $4\frac{1}{4}$ 4 $10\frac{1}{2}$ 5 $12\frac{3}{4}$

How to find a fraction of a quantity when the numerator is greater than 1

Example

Find $\frac{7}{10}$ of a metre. Give the answer in centimetres.

$\frac{1}{10}$ of a metre = $100 \div 10 = 10$ cm

$\frac{7}{10}$ of a metre = $10 \times 7 = 70$ cm

Example

Find $\frac{3}{5}$ of £30.25.

$\frac{1}{5}$ of £30.25 = £30.25 $\div$ 5 = £6.05

$\frac{3}{5}$ of £30.25 = £6.05 $\times$ 3 = £18.15

It is easy to remember, 'Divide by the bottom. Times by the top.'

How to compare fractions

Examples

Which is bigger, $\frac{7}{8}$ or $\frac{15}{16}$?

One way to compare fractions is to change one or more of them so that they have the same denominator. Here the **common denominator** can be 16. $\frac{7}{8} = \frac{14}{16}$ so $\frac{15}{16}$ is bigger.

How to change decimals to fractions

The first column after the decimal point contains tenths. $0.7 = \frac{7}{10}$

The second column after the decimal point is for hundredths. $0.07 = \frac{7}{100}$

Examples

$0.13 = \frac{13}{100}$ $0.12 = \frac{12}{100} = \frac{3}{25}$

The easy way to remember this is:
* write the decimal part of the number as a numerator, starting with the first non-zero digit after the point
* for the denominator, write 1 instead of the point and a zero for each of the given decimal places
* cancel if necessary.

Exercise 8

1 Find $\frac{3}{4}$ of £60.00.

2 In a sack of 120 potatoes, $\frac{3}{8}$ were mouldy. How many potatoes were mouldy?

3 $\frac{3}{4}$ of the pupils in a class went on a school trip. What fraction did not go?

4 Which is greater, and by how much, $\frac{1}{2}$ of 168 or $\frac{3}{4}$ of 108?

Exercise 9

Change these decimals to fractions.

1 0.1	2 0.5	3 0.25
4 0.75	5 0.16	6 0.005

How to change fractions to decimals

It is easy to change fractions to decimals if you remember that a fraction is another way of writing one number (the numerator) divided by another number (the denominator).

> **Example**
>
> $\frac{1}{2} = 1 \div 2$
>
> Write this as $1.0 \div 2$ and it is easier to see that the answer is 0.5.
> Sometimes you will need to add more than one zero. $\frac{3}{4} = 3.00 \div 4 = 0.75$

Recurring decimals

Sometimes the result of dividing the numerator by the denominator will go on for ever.
$\frac{1}{3} = 1 \div 3 = 0.333\,333\,3\ldots$ This is a recurring decimal.
When only one digit is involved, you usually write a dot above the recurring digit.
$0.333\,333\ldots$ is written as $0.\dot{3}$ and $0.177\,777\ldots$ becomes $0.1\dot{7}$.
If the repeating pattern involves two or more digits, you can write a bar over the top of the pattern, or use individual dots. $0.161\,616$ is written as $0.\overline{16}$ or $0.\dot{1}\dot{6}$.

How to compare fractions without using a common denominator

Sometimes a common denominator isn't obvious, or it would involve very large numbers. It may be easier to change the fractions to decimals.

> **Example**
>
> Which is greater, $\frac{11}{15}$ or $\frac{8}{11}$?
>
> $\frac{11}{15} = 11 \div 15 = 0.7\dot{3}$ and $\frac{8}{11} = 0.\dot{7}\dot{2}$ so $\frac{11}{15}$ is greater.

How to compare fractions, decimals and percentages

> **Examples**
>
> Arrange these numbers in order of size, smallest to largest. 0.3, 36%, $\frac{2}{5}$, $\frac{3}{8}$, 39%
> The easiest way is to change all the numbers into decimals. 0.3, 0.36, 0.4, 0.375, 0.39
> Then just rearrange the list. 0.3, 0.36, 0.375. 0.39, 0.4

Exercise 10

Change these fractions to decimals.

1 $\frac{5}{8}$ 2 $\frac{3}{10}$ 3 $\frac{2}{5}$ 4 $\frac{4}{5}$ 5 $\frac{3}{8}$

Exercise 11

Change these fractions to decimals.
Give your answers correct to 2 d.p.

1 $\frac{2}{3}$ 2 $\frac{3}{11}$ 3 $\frac{5}{9}$ 4 $\frac{3}{7}$ 5 $\frac{4}{9}$

Exercise 12

Write down the odd one out in each group.

1 0.6, $\frac{3}{5}$, 60%, $\frac{6}{10}$, 6%   2 0.625, $\frac{5}{8}$, 6.25, $\frac{15}{24}$, 62.5%   3 $\frac{7}{100}$, 0.07, 70%, 7%

Useful connections

All change!

Divide the numerator by the denominator.		Multiply by 100. Round to 2 d.p.
Fractions ⟶	Decimals ⟶	Percentages
Fraction	Decimal	%
$\frac{1}{2}$	0.5	50%
$\frac{1}{4}$	0.25	25%
$\frac{3}{4}$	0.75	75%
$\frac{1}{8}$	0.125	12.5% or 13% to nearest 1%
Fraction	Decimal	%
$\frac{1}{2}$	0.5	50%
$\frac{1}{10}$	0.1	10%
$\frac{1}{20}$	0.05	5%
$\frac{1}{100}$	0.01	1%
Fraction	Decimal	%
$\frac{1}{3}$	0.333…	$33\frac{1}{3}$% or 33% to nearest 1%
$\frac{2}{3}$	0.666…	$66\frac{2}{3}$% or 67% to nearest 1%

Exercise 13

Use the charts to help you to fill in the gaps.

1 a $\frac{3}{8}$ = _____ as a decimal = _____%   b $\frac{7}{8}$ = _____ as a decimal = _____%

  c $\frac{5}{8}$ = _____ as a decimal = _____%

2 a 50% = _____ as a decimal = _____ as a fraction.

  b $33\frac{1}{3}$% = _____ as a decimal = _____ as a fraction.

  c 5% = _____ as a decimal = _____ as a fraction.

3 a 0.1 = _____% = _____ as a fraction.   b 0.05 = _____% = _____ as a fraction.

  c 0.75 = _____% = _____ as a fraction.

Unit 5: Decimals, percentages and fractions

How to work out a percentage of an amount

The original whole amount is 100%.

> ### Example
> Jane cuts a cake into eight equal pieces. Her brother eats two of them.
> What percentage does he eat?
>
> 8 pieces = 100%   or   8 pieces = 100%
>
> 1 piece = 100 ÷ 8 = 12.5%   2 pieces = $\frac{1}{4}$ of 8 = 25%
>
> 2 pieces = 2 × 12.5% = 25%

> ### Example
> Mark buys five pizzas for a party and cuts them each into four equal pieces. The girls eat
> seven pieces, and the boys eat the rest. What percentage of the pizzas do the boys eat?
> The 5 pizzas will make 20 pieces. The boys eat 20 − 7 = 13 pieces.
>
> 20 pieces = 100%
>
> 1 piece = 5%
>
> 13 pieces = 65%

Exercise 14

Fill in the spaces.

1 a _____% is red.
   b _____% is blue.

2 a _____% is red.
   b _____% is blue.

3 a _____% is red.
   b _____% is blue.

4 a _____% is red.
   b _____% is blue.

①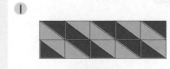

②

③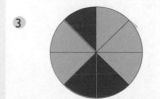

④

Using a scientific calculator

A scientific calculator always carries out operations in the following order:

1 **B** **B**rackets
2 **o** P**o**wer or r**o**ot
3 **D** **D**ivide
4 **M** **M**ultiply
5 **A** **A**dd
6 **S** **S**ubtract

BoDMAS?

Brackets

Using a scientific calculator, the answer to $3 + 2 \times 4$ is 11.

If you want to add the 3 and 2, then multiply the answer by 4, you can use brackets.

Calculator keyboards vary, but they will all have two bracket keys somewhere on the keyboard.

Work out $(3 + 2) \times 4$. Your answer should be 20.

Whenever you have a complicated calculation involving division, you can use brackets to help.

Example

$$\frac{36.78 + 87.91}{356.81 - 23.79}$$

Now work out the example in the following order:

$\boxed{(}\boxed{3}\boxed{6}\boxed{.}\boxed{7}\boxed{8}\boxed{+}\boxed{8}\boxed{7}\boxed{.}\boxed{9}\boxed{1}\boxed{)}\boxed{\div}\boxed{(}\boxed{3}\boxed{5}\boxed{6}\boxed{.}\boxed{8}\boxed{1}\boxed{-}\boxed{2}\boxed{3}\boxed{.}\boxed{7}\boxed{9}\boxed{)}\boxed{=}$

You can do this all in one go, without having to write down anything until the end.

$\dfrac{36.78 + 87.91}{356.81 - 23.79} = 0.37$ to 2 d.p.   Remember to press $\boxed{=}$ after closing the brackets.

Practise using the bracket keys until you are confident that you can use them correctly.

Exercise 1

Use a scientific calculator to do this exercise.

Give all answers correct to 2 d.p.

1 $46.9 + 17.23 \times 25.3 - 3.08$
2 $(46.9 + 17.23) \times (25.3 - 3.08)$
3 $67.4 - 4.76 \times 5.1 + 43.6$
4 $(67.4 - 4.76) \times (5.1 + 43.6)$

Powers are the small numbers that you see at the top and to the right of other numbers. RED

How to use powers or indices

It is likely that you will only need to raise numbers to the power of 2 or 3.
Raising a number to the power of 2 is squaring.
Raising a number to the power of 3 is cubing.
5^2 is 5×5 and is read as 'five squared'. 5^3 is $5 \times 5 \times 5$ and is read as 'five cubed'.

Two for the price of one! Using the SHIFT / 2ndF / INV keys

Most of the keys on a calculator have a number or symbol over them. To use this function and not the one on the key itself, press SHIFT , 2ndF or INV (usually placed at the top left-hand corner of the keyboard).
Some calculators have a separate key marked x^2 for squaring a number, but on others you will have to use SHIFT , 2ndF or INV as it shares a key with another function.

To cube a number, you may have to use the key marked x^y on some calculators and y^x on others.

> **Example**
> To work out 5^3, press 5 then x^y or y^x then 3 =
> Your calculator should display 125.

You can use x^y or y^x to work out any power, by substituting the required power for 3, but you will probably not need to do so at this stage. However, you could try it out for yourself, and check your answer by ordinary multiplication.

> **Example**
> To work out 7^6 press 7 then x^y or y^x then 6 =
> $7^6 = 7 \times 7 \times 7 \times 7 \times 7 \times 7 = 117649$

Exercise 2

Use a scientific calculator to do this exercise.
1 $3^3 \times 2^3$
2 Which is bigger, 5^8 or 8^5?

Tactics

Some calculators even give three functions per key. You will not need these functions yet, and you may never need some of them. If you want to find out about them, the information will be on the leaflet that came with the calculator.

3^4 is $3 \times 3 \times 3 \times 3$ and is read as 'three to the power of four' or 'three raised to the power of four'. The 4 is a *power* or an *index*.

RED ALERT

Shortcuts and easy methods

Shortcuts in adding and subtracting – rounding numbers

Example
Find the cost of 4 CDs at £9.99 each.
£9.99 is almost £10.00.
$4 \times £10.00 = £40.00$
But you have paid 1p too much on each CD.
£40.00 – 4p = £39.96

Example
£4.98 × 4
£4.98 is almost £5.00. The difference
is £0.02 or 2p.
$£5 \times 4 = £20.00$
£20.00 is (4 × 2p) too big.
$4 \times 2p = 8p$
£20.00 – £0.08 = £19.92

Example
412 + 97
97 is almost 100. The difference is 3.
$412 + 100 - 3 = 512 - 3 = 509$
$412 + 97 = 509$

Example
65 – 27
$\left.\begin{array}{l} 65 - 20 = 45 \\ 45 - 7 = 38 \end{array}\right\} \, 27 = 20 + 7$
$65 - 27 = 38$

Shortcuts in multiplying and dividing

Example
32 × 50
$32 \times 100 = 3200$
50 is $\frac{1}{2}$ of a hundred, so the solution is
$3200 \div 2 = 1600.$
$32 \times 50 = 1600$

Example
56 × 25
$56 \times 100 = 5600$
But 25 is $\frac{1}{4}$ of 100.
$5600 \div 4 = 1400$
$56 \times 25 = 1400$

Multiplying by 10 and 100 is covered on p10.

Exercise 1

Do not use a calculator to answer these questions.
1 £6.98 × 3
   (£6.98 is almost £7.00. The difference is £0.02 or 2p.)
2 24 × 25
3 £0.20 × 10
4 £8.99 × 6

Learning tables

If you can learn your multiplication tables up to at least 10×10, you will find maths much easier to understand and do. However, there are some people who just cannot remember them, and if you are one of those people, see if this idea works for you. Build on the framework as necessary.

Example

7×8

Most people can manage 1×8 and 10×8. Start by drawing a line as shown.

It is easy to build up 2×8 and 5×8.

$2 \times 8 + 1 \times 8 = 3 \times 8$

$2 \times 8 + 5 \times 8 = 7 \times 8$

8			8			8	
1	8		1	8		1	8
			2	16		2	16
						3	24
			5	40		5	40
						7	56
10	80		10	80		10	80

Easy table facts

- All even numbers are in the 2 times table.
- All numbers ending in 0 are in the 10 times table.
- All numbers ending in 5 or 0 are in the 5 times table.
- The digits of all numbers in the 9 times table add up to 9 (e.g. 18: 1 + 8, 54: 5 + 4).
- 7×8 and 8×7 are easy if you remember $56 = 7 \times 8$ (5, 6, 7, 8).
- Think of a clock face for the 15 times table: 15, 30, 45, 60.

Easy percentages

Some percentages are easy to work out without using a calculator.

Example

Work out 35% of £60.00.

10% = one-tenth, so 10% of £60.00 = £6.00

$5\% = \frac{1}{2}$ of 10%, so 5% of £60.00 = £3.00

$30\% = 3 \times 10\%$, so 30% of £60.00 = $3 \times £6.00 = £18.00$

35% of £60.00 = £18.00 + £3.00 = £21.00

Example

Work out 75% of 90.

50% of 90 = $\frac{1}{2}$ of 90 = 45

25% of 90 = $\frac{1}{4}$ of 90 = 22.5

75% of 90 = 45 + 22.5 = 67.5

Exercise 2

1 Work these out without using a calculator.
   a 15% of £160.00
   b 20% of £90.00
   c 399 + 199 + 99
   d 700 − 401
2 How many postcards at 25p each could you buy for £6.00?
   (Start by working out how many you could buy for £1.00.)

Tactics

You may be able to think up some quick methods of your own, but try several different examples to make sure they always work before you use them.

There are always plenty of ways of filling in the gaps in a multiplication table. Choose the one that appeals to you.

RED ALERT

Proportion

Understanding the jargon

Proportion is used to compare part of a group with the whole group. It is usually expressed as a fraction or a percentage.

> ### Example
>
> There are 24 pupils in a class: 18 are right-handed and 6 are left-handed.
>
> Then 18 out of a total of 24 are right-handed.
>
> The proportion of right-handed pupils is 18 out of 24, or $\frac{18}{24}$ or $\frac{3}{4}$ or 75%.
>
> The proportion of left-handed pupils is 6 out of 24 or $\frac{6}{24}$ or $\frac{1}{4}$ or 25%.

Proportions of quantities are measured as fractions, decimals or percentages.
If you are using fractions or decimals, the whole amount will add up to 1.
If you are using percentages, the whole amount will add up to 100%.

Exercise 1

1 In a class of 32 pupils, 0.75 have brown eyes and the rest have blue eyes.
   a What fraction of the class have blue eyes?
   b What fraction of the class have brown eyes?
   c What percentage of the class have brown eyes?
   d What percentage of the class have blue eyes?
   e How many pupils in the class have brown eyes?
   f How many pupils in the class have blue eyes?
2 Simon dilutes some fruit juice, so that the proportion of juice is 250 ml in every litre.
   How much juice is there in:
   a 1 litre   b 3 litres   c 2.5 litres?

Exercise 2

In a bag of 40 sweets, $\frac{1}{2}$ are toffees, $\frac{3}{8}$ are chocolates and the rest are jellies.

1 Work out the number of:
   a toffees   b chocolates   c jellies.
2 a What percentage are toffees?   b What percentage are either chocolates or jellies?
3 Complete the following.
   a 0.125 of the sweets are _____ .   b 0.375 of the sweets are _____ .

32

RED ALERT! **To cope with proportion and ratio questions, you need to be confident with fractions, decimals and percentages. Check out pages 20–28 before you go any further if you are at all unsure.**

Example

In a lucky dip tub, 10% of the prizes were puzzle books. 25% of the prizes were packets of crayons. 30% of the prizes were toy cars. 30% were small ornaments. The rest were bars of chocolate. There were 160 prizes altogether.

Complete the following sentences.

1 There were _____ books.
   You are told that 10% of the prizes were books.
   10% of 160 = 16. There were 16 books.

2 There were the same number of _____ and _____ .
   The question tells you that there were 30% of both cars and ornaments. There were the same number of toy cars and small ornaments.

3 There were _____ packets of crayons.
   25% of the prizes were packets of crayons.
   25% of 160 = 40

4 _____% of the prizes were bars of chocolate.
   10% + 25% + 30% + 30% of the prizes are accounted for, and the rest were chocolate bars. So 95% are accounted for, which means that there must be 5% chocolate bars.

5 There were _____ bars of chocolate.
   5% of the prizes were chocolate bars.
   5% of 160 = 8 There were 8 chocolate bars.

Exercise 3

1 What percentage of the diagram is pink?
2 What fraction of the diagram is blue?
3 What percentage of the diagram is either pink or blue?
4 What fraction of the diagram is not white?
5 What fraction of the diagram is either pink or black?

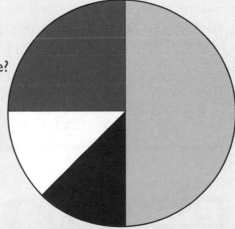

Exercise 4

The diagram shows a design for curtain fabric.
1 What fraction of the pattern shows leaves?
2 What percentage of the pattern shows flowers?

Percentages in a pie chart add up to 100%.
Degrees in a pie chart add up to 360°.   RED ALERT

Ratio

A ratio splits a group into parts, and compares the proportion of one part to another.

Example

There are 24 pupils in a class: 18 are right-handed and 6 are left-handed.
Then the ratio of right-handed to left-handed pupils is
18 right-handed to every 6 left-handed, written as 18 : 6 or 3 : 1.
So if the class were split into groups of four, in every group three pupils would be right-handed and one would be left-handed.

	Right-handed	Left-handed	Total number of pupils
1 group	3	1	4
2 groups	6	2	8
3 groups	9	3	12
4 groups	12	4	16
5 groups	15	5	20
6 groups	18	6	24

The ratio of right-handed to left-handed pupils is three to one or 3 : 1.
The ratio of left handed pupils to right handed pupils is one to three or 1 : 3.

If there is 1 adult for every 8 pupils on a trip, the ratio of adults to pupils is 1 : 8.
If there are 8 pupils for every 1 adult on a trip, the ratio of pupils to adults is 8 : 1.

How to work out a ratio

Example

Share £45.00 between Barry and Harry in the ratio 1 : 2.
Imagine the money is put into bags, with the same amount
of money in each bag.
Barry receives one bag. Harry receives two bags.
There are 1 + 2 = 3 bags altogether.
In each bag, there will be £45 ÷ 3 = £15.00
Barry will receive 1 × £15.00 = £15.00 and Harry will receive 2 × £15.00 = £30.00.

Exercise 1

On a school trip, one adult is to be responsible for five pupils.

1 a If 1 adult goes, 1 × 5 = 5 pupils can go.
   b If 2 adults go, _____ pupils can go.
   c If 3 adults go, _____ pupils can go.
   d If 9 adults go, _____ pupils can go.

2 a If 5 pupils go, 5 ÷ 5 = 1 adult will be required.
   b If 10 pupils go, _____ adults will be required.
   c If 15 pupils go, _____ adults will be required
   d If 45 pupils go, _____ adults will be required.

3 There is 1 adult for every 5 pupils. The ratio of adults to pupils is _____ .
4 There are 5 pupils for every 1 adult. The ratio of pupils to adults is _____ .

It is very important to keep the numbers in the same order as the words when writing a ratio in figures. RE

Example

Surinder is making brown paint by mixing red, green and blue paint in the ratio 4 : 2 : 2.
How much of each colour will he need to make 24 litres of paint?
Imagine the 24 litres poured into equal-sized tins.

He will have 4 + 2 + 2 = 8 tins.
Each tin will contain 24 ÷ 8 = 3 litres.
4 × 3 = 12 litres of red, 4 × 2 = 8 litres of green and 4 × 2 = 8 litres of blue.

Example

Great aunt Matilda gave some money to Suzanne and Paul in the ratio of their ages, 3 : 2.
a   If Suzanne received £90.00, how much did Paul receive?
b   How much money did she give to the two children altogether?

Imagine that the money was put into bags, with the same amount in each bag.

You already know that Suzanne had three bags and that she received £90.00.
Therefore, there must be £90.00 ÷ 3 = £30.00 in each bag.
a   Paul received 2 × £30.00 = £60.00.
b   The total amount that she gave the children was £90.00 + £60.00 = £150.00.

Exercise 2

1   Lucy was doing a project on traffic. She found that in half an hour, on one morning,
    72 cars and 6 buses passed the school.
    a   Write this as a ratio cars : buses in its simplest form.
    b   If 18 buses had passed the school, how many cars would
        have passed, assuming the ratio stayed the same?
2   Jonathan's test results for geography and history were
    in the ratio 2 : 3. If he scored 64% for geography,
    what did he score for history?
3   Share £300 among Pat, Paul and Peter in the ratio of
    the number of letters in their names.

Tactics

You can write ratios
with a colon instead
of 'to'.
Always give your answer
in its simplest form,
unless you are told
otherwise.

35

Algebra basics

Understanding the jargon

Evaluate find the value of (If you evaluate $3 + 4$, you should get the answer 7.)
Expression a group of numbers or letters that forms part of an equation or a fomula
Simplify an expression find the total of all the different variables and the total of any numbers which you have (This sounds complicated, but is really quite easy, see page 39.)

Variables

In algebra, letters are often used to stand for numbers. These do not necessarily have a fixed value, but may vary. They are called variables. This will be easier to understand when you have worked through pages 36–41.

How to write algebra

Adding and subtracting
Write addition and subtraction in the same way as usual, for example, $a + b$, $y - x$ and so on.

Multiplying
Because the letter x is frequently used as the variable, it could easily be mistaken for a multiplication sign. You can avoid this confusion by leaving out the multiplication sign.
For $a \times b$ or $b \times a$, write ab.
For $a \times 3$ or $3 \times a$, write $3a$.
It would also be correct to write $a3$, but you usually start with the number.
For $a \times 1$, write a.
A variable on its own means $1 \times$ that variable.
$2a + 3b$ means $(2 \times a) + (3 \times b)$.

Dividing
Division is usually written in fraction form.
For $a \div b$, write $\dfrac{a}{b}$.

Exercise 1

1 Write these algebraically.
    a $2 \times c$ **b** $p \times q$ **c** $3 \div d$ **d** $n \div 5$ **e** $m \div n$

2 Is cd the same as dc?

3 Is $\dfrac{c}{d}$ the same as $\dfrac{d}{c}$?

Unit 10: Algebra basics

How to write a formula or statement

Example
a Maria is 12 years old. Her brother is four years older. How old is her brother?
b How old was her brother when Maria was six years old?
c If you know how old Maria is, how can you work out how old her brother is?
a 12 + 4 = 16
b 6 + 4 = 10
c Add 4 to Maria's age. You can write this algebraically. Choose a letter to represent Maria's

Suppose Maria has a sister who is three years younger than she is.
If you know Maria's age, you can work out how old her sister is by subtracting 3 years from it.
Alternatively, you can write this as $m - 3$.

Example
John is four years old. Arif is twice as old as John. Daniel is three years older than Arif.
How old are Arif and Daniel?
Arif is $2 \times 4 = 8$ years old.
Daniel is $2 \times 4 + 3 = 11$ years old.

Example
a Work out the ages of Arif and Daniel if John is seven years old.
b Work out the ages of Arif and Daniel if John is n years.
a Arif is $2 \times 7 = 14$ years old.
   Daniel is $2 \times 7 + 3 = 17$ years old.
b Arif is $2 \times n = 2n$ years old.

Example
a Jane is 12 years old. Ian is $\frac{1}{2}$ her age. How old is Ian?
b If Jane is y years old, how old is Ian?
a Ian is $12 \div 2$ or $\frac{12}{2} = 6$ years old.

Answers like $m - 3$ or $2n + 4$, are algebraic expressions. The examples above tell you how to work out an age, so they are formulae.

Exercise 2

1 Tom has ten sweets. His friend has two more sweets than he has. How many sweets does his friend have?
2 Jack has s sweets. His sister has two more sweets than he has. How many sweets does his sister have?
3 Owen has eight sweets. His brother has w sweets more than he does. How many sweets does his brother have?
4 Anna is eight years old. Her brother is twice as old as she is. How old is her brother?
5 Rebecca is b years old. Her sister is twice as old as she is. How old is her sister?
6 Rebecca's brother is two years younger than Rebecca's sister. How old is her brother?

Using brackets

You use brackets when you need to do one operation before another, or you need to describe two or more separate operations.

> **Example**
> Start with a number, n. Multiply it by 3 and then add 1.
> Write a formula for the result.

> **Example**
> Start with a number, n. Subtract 2 and multiply the result by 4.
> Write a formula to show this.

In algebra it is usual to leave out the multiplication sign, and write $4(n - 2)$ instead of $(n - 2) \times 4$. It would be correct to write $(n - 2)4$, but it is more usual to write it as $4(n - 2)$.

How to write square numbers

Start with a number, n.
- Multiply it by itself: $n \times n$ or n^2
- Multiply your answer by 3: $3n^2$

Start with a number, n.
- Multiply it by 3: $3n$
- Square your answer: $(3n)^2 = 3n \times 3n = 9n^2$

How to evaluate expressions

To evaluate means to find the value.
If $a = 3$, then $a + a + a + a + a = 3 + 3 + 3 + 3 + 3 = 5$ lots of 3, or 5×3 or 15.

> **Examples**
> $a = 2$, $b = 5$, and $c = 3$.
> - $a + b - c = 2 + 5 - 3 = 4$
> - $(b \times c) - a = (5 \times 3) - 2 = 15 - 2 = 13$

Exercise 3

1 Which of the following is equal to n^2?
   $n + n, n \times n, 2 \times n$

2 Which of the following is the same as adding three to a number, n, and doubling the result?
   $3 + (n \times 2), \quad 3 + n \times 2, \quad (3 + n) \times 2, \quad 3n \times 2, \quad 2(3 + n)$

3 Work out the value of each expression, taking $x = 4, y = 2, z = 1$.
   a $2x + y$
   b $x - z$
   c $y^2 - z$
   d $(x + y) \div (y + z)$
   e $5(x - z)$
   f $\dfrac{y}{2} + x^2$

If you knew a value for n, and were working out the answer on a scientific calculator, the brackets would be ve important. If you leave out the brackets in $(n - 2) \times 4$, and let $n = 5$, a basic calculator would work out $5 - 2 = 3$ $3 \times 4 = 12$, so the final answer would be 12. See what happens if you work out $5 - 2 \times 4$ with a scientific calcula

How to simplify expressions

Simplify expressions by grouping together all the similar variables and all the numbers.

$a + a + a + a + a = 5a$

In the expression $5 + s + 3 + s$, the numbers $5 + 3$ belong together and the $s + s$ belong together.

$5 + s + 3 + s = 5 + 3 + s + s = 8 + 2s$

If $s = 5$, $s^2 = 25$ and $s + s^2 = 30$, $3s = 15$ and $s^3 = 5 \times 5 \times 5 = 125$.

Example

Simplify the following expressions where possible. Remember, a variable on its own without a number in front means $1 \times$ that variable. $y = 1 \times y$

a	$y + y + y$	$y + y + y = 3y$
b	$a + 2a + a$	$a + 2a + a = 4a$
c	$l + w + l + w$	$l + w + l + w = 2(l + w)$ or $l + l + w + w = 2l + 2w$
d	$2w + 2 + w^2$	$2w + 2 + w^2$ will not simplify.
e	$c + 4 + 2c + 3c$	$c + 4 + 2c + 3c = c + 2c + 3c + 4 = 6c + 4$

How to write equations

Think of a number, n, multiply it by 2 and add 3. You can write this as a formula:

$2n + 3$.

If the result of this calculation is 13, this can be written as an equation:

$2n + 3 = 13$.

Example

The cost of a book is d pounds.
The total cost of three of these books is $3d$ pounds.
The total cost is T pounds.
$3d = T$
If the total cost of these 3 books is £30.00, then $3d = £30.00$.

Example

The total amount of money in Mel's purse is T pence.
The cost of a pen is r pence, so the cost of 6 pens is $6r$.
If Mel buys 6 pens and has 80p left, then the amount of money that she had to start with is $6r + 80$.

Exercise 4

Complete these.

1   The number of wheels on a toy car is 4. The number of wheels on h toy cars is … .
    If there are h toy cars and 3 wheels left over, then the total number of wheels (T) is … .
    $T = \ldots + \ldots$

2   Pupils were collecting vouchers for school equipment.
    The total number of vouchers was V.
    20 pupils collected k vouchers each. $V = \ldots$
    75 vouchers were lost, so the number of vouchers available was … . $V = \ldots$

3   A CD cost £9.99 Imran bought t CDs, so the amount in pounds which he spent was … .
    He still had £4.54 left over. He started with m pounds, so $9.99t + 4.54 = \ldots$

RT   You can only group like with like. You cannot simplify $s + s^2$ as s and s^2 are different. $s + s^2$ is not the same as s^3 or $3s$.   ALERT

How to solve equations

In the last exercise you practised forming equations.
More usually, you are given the equation and you have to solve it.

How to use a function machine
Machine 1
Let your starting number be x and your
finishing number be 9.
Then the equation is $x + 3 = 9$.

Machine 2
Let your starting number be y and your
finishing number be 15.
Then $y \times 2 - 1 = 15$, or $2y - 1 = 15$.

Machine 3
Let your starting number be z and your
finishing number be 9.
Then $\frac{z}{3} + 5 = 9$.

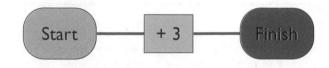

You can go back to the beginning in a function machine by carrying out an inverse operation.
$+$ and $-$ are inverse operations. You can 'undo' addition by subtracting, and
you can undo subtraction by adding. The inverse of addition is subtraction,
and the inverse of subtraction is addition.
$3 \times 2 = 6 \quad 6 \div 2 = 3$ or $6 \div 3 = 2$
You can undo multiplying by dividing, and you can undo dividing by
multiplying. The inverse of multiplication is division, and the inverse of division is multiplication.
Adding an amount sends the total in one direction. Subtracting the same amount sends it back
to where it started.
Dividing by an amount sends the total in one direction. Multiplying by the same amount sends
it back to where it started.

> **Example**
> $6 + 4 = 10$

Exercise 1

Solve the three equations described above:

1 $x + 3 = 9$
2 $2y - 1 = 15$
3 $\frac{z}{3} + 5 = 9$

To solve the equation using the inverse of function machine 1, subtract 3 from the answer.

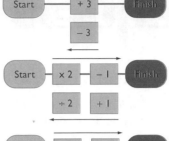

To solve the equation using the inverses of function machine 2, add 1 to the answer and then divide by 2.

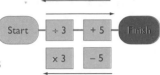

To solve the equation using the inverses of function machine 3, subtract 5 from the answer and multiply the result by 3.

You can solve equations without using function machines

Example

I think of a number: x
I add 3: $x + 3$
The result is 12: $x + 3 = 12$
What was my original number?
Before I added 3, I started with $12 - 3$.

Example

I started with a number: y
I multiplied it by 3: $3y$
The result was 15. $3y = 15$
What was my original number?
Before I multiplied by 3.

Example

I started with a number:
g
I multiplied it by 5: $5g$
I subtracted 1: $5g - 1$
The result was 9: $5g - 1 = 9$
What was my original number?
$5g - 1 = 9$ (The inverse of + is −.)
$5g = 9 + 1$
$5g = 10$ (The inverse of × is ÷.)

Example

I started with a number: w
I divided it by 2: $\dfrac{w}{2}$
I added 6: $\dfrac{w}{2} + 6$

The result was 11. $\dfrac{w}{2} + 6 = 11$
What was my original number?
$\dfrac{w}{2} + 6 = 11$
$\dfrac{w}{2} = 11 - 6 = 5$
$\dfrac{w}{2} = 5$ so $w = 5 \times 2 = 10$
$w = 10$

Exercise 2

Solve these equations.
1 $y + 4 = 13$
2 $r - 2 = 18$
3 $2t = 18$
4 $3f + 4 = 19$
5 $2x - 1 = 13$

Tactics

An inverse operation is rather like running back through a video. People who are coming into a room when the video is running forwards, go backwards out of the room when you rewind.

Sequences

Understanding the jargon

Sequence a list of numbers which form a pattern according to a given rule
Term a number in a sequence (The first number is the first term, the next is the second term ...)
Consecutive numbers that follow each other without a gap, like 1, 2, 3, ...

How to work out sequence patterns

> ### Example
> You find the number of matchsticks in the next pattern by adding on 2 each time.
>
> | Pattern | 1 | 2 | 3 |
> |---|---|---|---|
> | Number of matchsticks | 3 | 5 | 7 |

Draw the next two patterns on the diagram. Check that the fourth pattern has **9** matchsticks and the fifth pattern has **11** matchsticks.

If you know the rule, you can work out the number of matchsticks you need for any pattern in the sequence without having to count on each time.

Exercise 1

Pattern number

 1   2   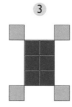 3

Fill in the gaps in the sentences.

1 The number of red squares is $p \times$ _____
2 The number of blue squares is always _____
3 The total number of squares is $2p$ _____ 4.

Pattern number (p)	Number of red squares (r)	Number of blue squares (b)	Total (t)
1	2	4	6
2	4	4	8
3	6	4	10

Exercise 2

Fill in the next two numbers in each sequence. explain why you chose these numbers.

1 4, 7, 10, 13, 16, ..., ...
2 1, 4, 9, 16, 25, ..., ...
3 22, 18, 14, 10, ..., ...

How to use a formula – the fast track to forming sequences

> ### Example
>
> | Position | 1st | 2nd | 3rd | 4th | ... |
> |----------|-----|-----|-----|-----|-----|
> | Term | 5 | 8 | 11 | 14 | ... |
>
> In this sequence, the first term is 5, the second term is 8, the third term is 11 and so on.
> If we wanted to find, for instance, the 29th term although we could do it by continuing to add 3, there is an easier and quicker way.
> In this sequence, n stands for the position of the term which you need to find.
> The formula for this sequence, i.e. the formula to find the nth term is $t = 3n + 2$.

Check that the formula works for the third and fourth terms.
Use the formula to find the fifth and sixth terms. You should have the answers 17 and 20.
To find the 29th term, replace n by 29. The 29th term is $3 \times 29 + 2 = 89$.

You can use flowcharts to make sequences

> ### Example
> Write the first three terms of the sequence which follows the rule $t = n + 3$.
> If $n = 1$, $t = 1 + 3 = 4$ If $n = 2$, $t = 2 + 3 = 5$

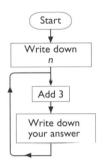

Exercise 3

1 Write the first three terms of the sequence which follows the rule $t = n - 1$.
2 Write the first three terms of a sequence which follows the rule $t = 2n + 1$
3 Write the first three terms of a sequence which follows the rule $t = n^2 + 1$
4 The nth term is $2n + 3$
  Fill in the gaps.

Position	1	2	3	4	5	6	7	8	9	10
Term	5	7								

Exercise 4

1 Write down all the terms of this sequence, with a starting number of 3. The first two terms have been done for you. 3, 7
2 How many terms are in the sequence?
3 Now make a sequence using the same flowchart, starting from 6.
4 How many terms does this sequence have?

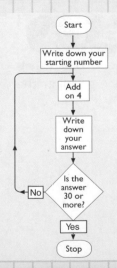

Finding the formula for a sequence is often called finding the nth term.

RT   ALERT

Graphs

Understanding the jargon

Axes a horizontal line, usually referred to as the x-axis, and a vertical line, the y-axis
Origin the point (0, 0) where the axes cross
Coordinates pair of numbers that describe the position of a point on a grid

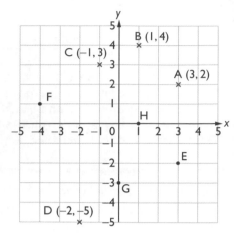

Understanding graphs

Any point on a graph may be located by its position in relation to the point where the axes cross (the origin). The position is given as a value across and a value up or down the graph. For instance, point A is at (3, 2) and point B is at (1, 4). These values are the coordinates.

The first number is the x-coordinate and the second number is the y-coordinate. Coordinates can be positive or negative. C is at (−1, 3) and D is at (−2, −5).

The axes divide the graph into four regions, each of which is called a **quadrant**. The top right-hand quadrant is the first quadrant.

How to fill in tables of values

Example

$y = x + 3$ This equation means that the y-value is always 3 more than the x-value.

x	0	1	2	3	4	5	6
$y = x + 3$	3	4	5	6	7	8	9

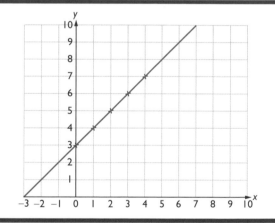

Exercise 1

1 Write down the coordinates of these points on the graph at the top of the page:
E, F, G, H

Tactics

Remember that the x-axis is the line $y = 0$ and the y-axis is the line $x = 0$

Always read across the graph, for the
x-coordinate, before
reading up or down for the y-coordinate.

RED A   ED

You should always label the axes and the equation line.

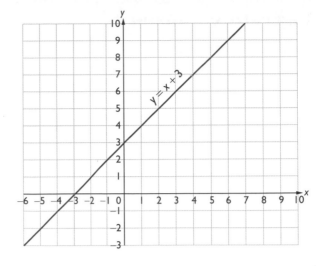

Reading graphs

You can use graphs to answer questions about the information they display. Always draw graphs as accurately as you can. To find other values of x and y from this graph, simply insert the information for either x or y and draw a straight line from the point you have chosen to the line of the graph. Then draw another line joining that point to the other axis, and read off the value.

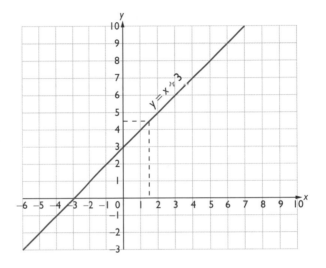

From this graph, the two lines meet at (1.5, 4.5), so when x is 1.5, y is 4.5.

Exercise 2

1 Draw a set of axes, labelling the x-axis from −4 to 4 and the y-axis from −12 to 12.

2 Complete these tables of values.

a
x	0	1	2	3	4
y = x	0				

b
x	0	1	2	3	4
y = 2x	0				

c
x	0	1	2	3	4
y = 3x	0				

3 Mark each pair of coordinates of y = x and join the points with a straight line. Extend the line beyond the given points. Do the same for y = 2x and y = 3x.

RT RED ALERT RED ALERT! RED ALERT RED ALERT

Discrete variables

Look at this pattern.

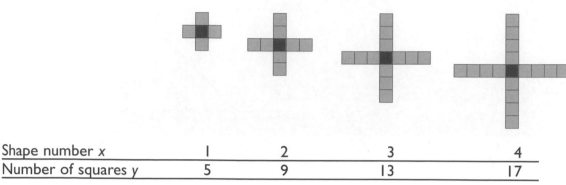

Shape number x	1	2	3	4
Number of squares y	5	9	13	17

The graph on the right shows the information in the table.
You do not join up the points on this type of graph. It would be
silly to try to find out how many squares there are for shape
number 3.5, for example, because the shape number has to be a
whole number. The same is true if one of the variables is the
number of children in a family, or the number of cars in a
showroom.

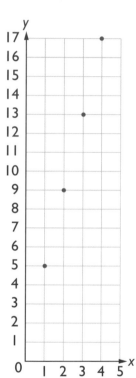

Exercise 3

1 Fill in the table of values for $y = x + 5$.

x	0	1	2	3	4	5	6
$y = x + 5$	5	6					

2 Use squared paper. Draw a set of axes, labelling the x-axis from -3 to 6
and the y-axis from -3 to 10, and draw the graph of $y = x + 5$.
Remember to label the equation line.
3 Draw lines on your graph to find y when $x = -2$.
4 Draw lines on your graph to find x when $y = 6.5$

Sometimes you will see graph points joined up, to make the shape of the
graph show up more clearly.

How to use everyday graphs

Graphs can be used to show journeys, as in the next example, or to show relationships between two measures, as in the exercise.

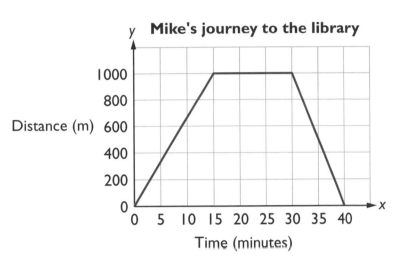

Mike's journey to the library

Example

One morning, Mike went to the library to return a book.
The *x*-axis shows the time he took, in minutes.
The *y*-axis shows the distance he went, in metres.
a How far is the library from Mike's home?
b How long did he take to get there?
c How long did he stay at the library?
d How long did he take to get home?
a The journey from Mike's home to the library is shown by the first part of the graph.
   The line straightens out at 1000 m, so the library is 1 km away.
b 15 minutes
c This is the part of the graph where the distance stayed the same. He was in the library
   for 15 minutes.
d 10 minutes.

Exercise 4

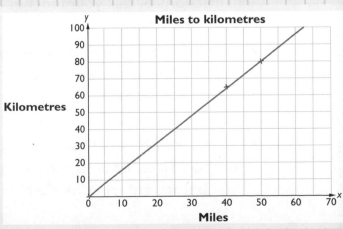

Miles to kilometres

This graph shows an approximate conversion between kilometres and miles. Use the information on the graph to answer the questions. Draw lines on the graph to help you.
I If you were travelling at 50 miles per hour, roughly how fast would you be travelling in kilometres per hour?
2 If you went for a distance of 65 kilometres, roughly how far would you have gone in miles?

47

2

Things to do: choose a calculator

- When you decide you want a calculator, make sure that the one you buy is the one you need.

  - Different manufacturers use different keying methods and different keyboard layouts, and new models of calculator are constantly coming out. Your school may recommend a particular model of calculator – if so, go with the flow. Your teacher may explain a process to the class, assuming that everyone has the same machine. Life could be very difficult if yours is different.

  - If your school does not have a scheme, ask your teacher to recommend a calculator. In any case, *make sure you buy a scientific one* that does the operations in the same way that the majority of mathematicians all over the world do!

  - Your calculator may have $\boxed{\text{STO}}$ (store) and $\boxed{\text{RCL}}$ (recall keys) or $\boxed{\text{Min}}$ (memory in) and $\boxed{\text{MR}}$ (memory recall) keys. Most have $\boxed{\text{M+}}$ for adding to what is already stored. Some calculators have more than one memory. To clear a memory, simply enter zero into it. You may prefer to use a memory for some processes instead of brackets. Again, read the instructions or ask your teacher to help you. Not all calculators use the same procedure.

  - Most calculators have at least one fraction key, and some have several. Fraction keys are always marked with a fraction, but written in letters instead of numbers. Letters may be capital or lower case. Your calculator may have $\boxed{^a/_b}$, or $\boxed{A^B/c}$, or it may use other letters such as x and y.

  - The $\boxed{^+/_-}$ key is very useful for changing a positive number into a negative number. To enter a negative number, you may need to press $\boxed{^+/_-}$ before entering the number, or afterwards.

48

- Make sure you can find the square root $\boxed{\sqrt{}}$ key. If you have a separate key with $\boxed{x^2}$, it is probably next to it. If not, you will probably need the $\boxed{\text{SHIFT}}$, $\boxed{\text{2ndF}}$, or $\boxed{\text{INV}}$ key.

Once you have bought your calculator, there are a few things you should remember.

- Look after the instructions.
- Find a safe way of carrying your calculator around at school. Calculators do not like being dropped. Nor is it a good idea to get them wet.
- Keep your calculator in its case. It's less likely to get damaged.
- Practise using your calculator. Try out unfamiliar processes using small numbers, so that you can tell if you have the right answer.
- If your calculator is battery-operated, find out how to replace the battery, and do it as soon as you need to.

Other maths hardware

The special equipment that you will certainly need for maths includes a ruler, a pair of compasses and possibly a set square. It is a good idea to buy tins or cases of mathematical instruments, because you then have somewhere safe to keep everything and you can see at a glance if anything is missing. Carrying a pair of compasses around can be quite dangerous if you just put it in the bottom of your bag – both to you and to other people.

Organise your time

Try to get into the habit of packing your bag the night before. This can seem a real chore if you are tired, or planning a night out, but it really does save a great deal of stress, especially if you can't find last night's homework in the morning scramble. Teachers take a dim view of homework which is handed in late without a good reason, and you really don't want to start getting detentions. You have better things to do with your time!

Keep homework under control. Quite often year 7 students are set work which has to be handed in the next day, but sometimes teachers set work several days in advance. Write a reminder note in your homework diary or work planner several days before the due date, so that you aren't struck by a nasty, last minute surprise.

Measurement

How to change from one metric unit to another

Length

$$\text{mm} \xrightarrow{\div 10} \text{cm} \xrightarrow{\div 100} \text{m} \xrightarrow{\div 1000} \text{km}$$
$$\text{mm} \xleftarrow{\times 10} \text{cm} \xleftarrow{\times 100} \text{m} \xleftarrow{\times 1000} \text{km}$$

This is an easy way to change from one unit to another.
(If you have forgotten how to multiply or divide decimals by 10, 100 or 1000, look back to page 10.)

Example
Change 5432 mm to m.
5432 mm ÷ 10 = 543.2 cm
543.2 cm ÷ 100 = 5.432 m

Example
Change 1.2 km to centimetres.
1.2 km × 1000 = 1200 m
1200 m × 100 = 120 000 cm

Example
Change 15 000 000 cm to km.
15 000 000 cm ÷ 100 000 = 150 km

You can use the same idea with capacity and mass.

How to measure volume or capacity
Volume is measured in cubic centimetres.
These are written as cm^3.
$1\ cm^3 = 1$ millilitre, usually written as 1 ml
1000 ml = 1 litre

$$\text{m}l \xrightarrow{\div 1000} l$$
$$\text{m}l \xleftarrow{\times 1000} l$$

Exercise 1

1 Write these measurements in cm.
   a 152 mm b 21 mm c 5 mm
   d 1.8 m   e 32 m   f 453 m
2 Write these measurements in the units in brackets.
   a 36 cm (m)   b 36 cm (mm) c 45 cm (m)
   d 4250 cm (km)   e 735 m (km)   f 21 462 m (km)

How to measure weight or mass

As any scientist will tell you, weight and mass are not exactly the same but, at this stage you do not need to worry about the difference. For questions on weight or mass, use grams, kilograms or tonnes.

grams $\xrightarrow{\div 1000}$ kg $\xrightarrow{\div 1000}$ tonnes

$\times 1000$ $\times 1000$

These are easy since you only have to remember to multiply or divide by 1000 each time.

Imperial units

You do not need to learn these, but it is useful to know rough equivalents for metric and imperial measures.

A yard used to be the distance between the reigning monarch's nose and the tip of his thumb, with arm outstretched. Not a lot of people know that!

Length

12 inches = 1 foot
3 feet = 1 yard
1760 yards = 1 mile
30 cm is about 1 foot
1 m is just over 1 yard
A kilometre is about $\frac{5}{8}$ miles

Capacity

2 pints = 1 quart
4 quarts = 1 gallon
1 gallon is about $4\frac{1}{2}$ litres

Weight or mass

16 ounces = 1 pound   The abbreviation for ounce is oz, and the abbreviation for pound is lb. So 16 oz = 1 lb

14 pounds = 1 stone
1 kg is approximately 2.2 lb. If you have to work out an approximate weight, changing between kilograms and pounds, without a calculator, use the approximation 1 kg $\approx$ 2 lb.

Exercise 2

1 Write these capacities in the units in brackets.
   a 4 litres (ml)   b 3.5 litres (ml)   c 7.2 litres (ml)
   d 450 ml (litres)   e 2163 ml (litres)
   f 723 ml (litres)
2 Fill in the missing words. Do not use a calculator to work out the answers.
   a 6 lbs are about .... kg.
   b 9 litres are about .... gallons.
   c 20 km are about .... miles.

Tactics

The same method works for all the metric units – just keep multiplying or dividing by powers of 10. 'Journey's end is full of smiles 8 kilometres make 5 miles.'

RT RED **The sign $\approx$ means 'is approximately equal to'.** ALERT RED

Angles and lines

Understanding the jargon

Angle amount or turn where two (or more) lines meet

Vertex corner where two lines or three edges meet

Vertices corners

Intersect cross – lines that cross each other are intersecting lines

Intersection the point where two lines cross

Equidistant the same distance from each other

Parallel lines that are always equidistant (Spelling hint: The two letter ls in the word 'parallel' are parallel lines.)

Perpendicular meeting or intersecting at right angles

Interior angle the angle inside the vertex of a shape

Exterior angle the angle at the vertex of a shape, where one side is extended outside the shape

Congruent identical in shape and size (You can fit congruent shapes on top of one another, although you may have to turn one of them over or round to do so.)

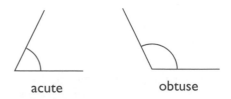
acute   obtuse

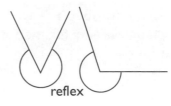
reflex

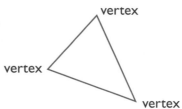
vertex   vertex   vertex

A triangle has three vertices.

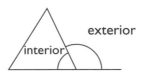
interior   exterior

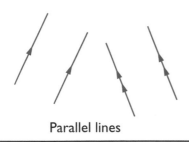
Parallel lines

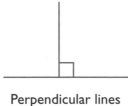
Perpendicular lines at right angles (90°)

Intersecting lines

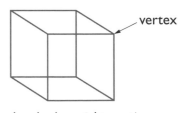
vertex

A cube has eight vertices.

Exercise 1

1   Look at each of these angles and write down which type it is.

    a   b   c   d   e

2   Which pairs of lines are parallel? Which are perpendicular?

    a   b   c   d   e

Labelling shapes

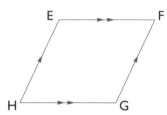

This line is called AB or BA.

A ——————— B

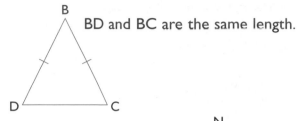

BD and BC are the same length.

EF and HG are parallel, and EH and FG are parallel.

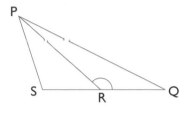

MN and NJ are the same length, and MJ = JK = KL = ML.

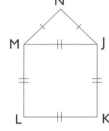

Labelling angles

When it is not clear which angle is being referred to, use the three-letter notation. The angle marked on the triangle cannot be simply called angle R, because there are three angles at the point R. The sides PR and QR meet at R, so the angle is called angle PRQ or angle QRP. You may also see angles written with symbols, like this: ∠PRQ or P̂RQ.

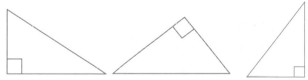

Labelling right angles
Angles of 90° are right angles. They are marked on diagrams as shown below.

Types of triangle

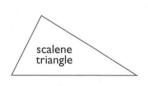

scalene triangle

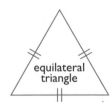

equilateral triangle

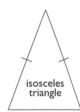

isosceles triangle

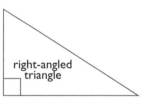

right-angled triangle

Exercise 2

1 Name the angles marked using 3 letter notation.

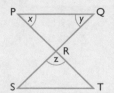

Tactics

Remember the different types of triangle. Equilateral triangles have three angles of 60°. An isosceles right-angled triangle has two angles of 45°.

2 Describe this triangle fully.

Be warned when it states beside the diagram, 'Shape not accurately drawn' or 'Diagram not drawn to scale'. Don't try to find the answer by measuring.

Lines and angles

Angles *a* and *b* are adjacent angles.

$a + b = 180°$

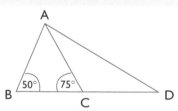

$c + d + e = 180°$

Angles on a straight line add up to 180°.

Angles round a point add up to 360°.

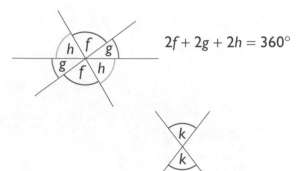

$2f + 2g + 2h = 360°$

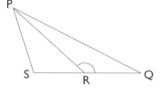

The two angles marked *k* are vertically opposite angles.

Interior and exterior angles
The exterior angle of a triangle = the sum of the two opposite interior angles.

$\angle PRQ = \angle RPS + \angle RSP$
$\angle PRS = \angle RPQ + \angle RQP$

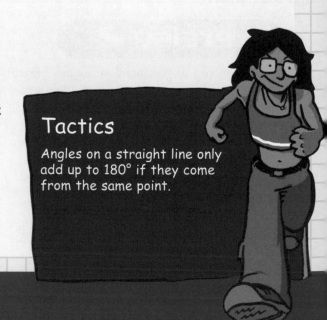

Exercise 3

In the diagram, which is not accurately drawn, $\angle ACB = 75°$ and $\angle ABC = 50°$.

1 Work out the size of:
   a $\angle BAC$
   b $\angle ACD$
   c $\angle ABC + \angle BAC$.
2 Now repeat question 1, making $\angle ACB = 49°$ and $\angle ABC = 61°$.
3 Make up some more examples, using different values for $\angle ACB$ and $\angle ABC$.
   What do you notice about $\angle ACD$ and $\angle ABC + \angle BAC$?

Tactics

Angles on a straight line only add up to 180° if they come from the same point.

Alternate angles

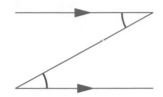
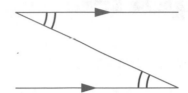

You may know angles like the ones marked in the diagram below as z angles but their correct name is alternate angles.

Corresponding angles

You may know angles like the ones in the diagram below as F angles, but their correct name is corresponding angles.

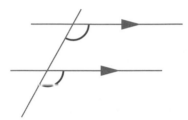
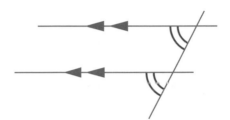

Exercise 4

QST, RSUV and WUT are straight lines.
Use three-letter notation to describe all the angles in this question.

1   Name an angle which is equal to ∠QSR.
2   Give another name for **a** ∠SUT **b** ∠UWV.
3   Name one angle in the shape which is definitely a right angle.
4   Name an angle vertically opposite to ∠SUT.
5   Which side is parallel to XW?
6   Which side is the same length as RS?
7   Name an angle which is:
    a   alternate to ∠XSU
    b   corresponding to∠XSU.
8   Name all the angles which meet at S.

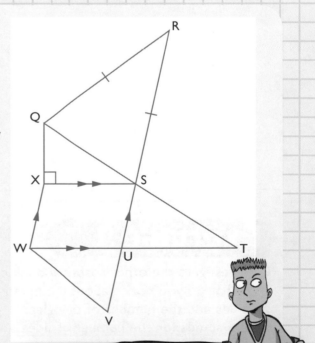

Tactics

The exterior angle of a triangle is formed by extending one of the sides. Draw a triangle and check how many exterior angles you can make.

Polygons

Understanding the jargon

Polygon any two-dimensional straight-sided shape
Regular polygon a polygon where all sides are of the same length
All the interior angles of a regular polygon are the same size.

Interior angles of polygons

Draw a square, and join the diagonal from one vertex (corner), as in the diagram.
How many triangles have you made?

Now do the same, using a
five-sided shape, i.e. a pentagon.
Remember, you only join the
diagonals from one vertex.

You can put the results in a table.

Number of sides S	Number of triangles T
4	2
5	3
6	
7	
8	
9	
10	

Exercise 1

1 Investigate the other shapes and fill in the chart above.
2 What do you notice about the number of
   sides and the number of triangles?
3 If S stands for the number of sides, and
   T stands for the number of triangles,
   write a formula to find the number of
   triangles in a shape if you know the
   number of sides.

Tactics

A shape that is not
symmetrical is asymmetrical.
A trapezium can be symmetrical
or asymmetrical.

The sum of the interior angles of a shape

You find the sum of the interior angles of a polygon by adding together all the interior angles.
An easy way to do this is to use the fact that the angle sum of any triangle is 180°.
Just multiply this by the number of triangles you make.
The angles of a square or rectangle add up to 360°, because $4 \times 90° = 360°$. You can also show
that the angles of any quadrilateral (four-sided shape) add up to 360°.
Use the answers to Exercise 1 to complete this table. Fill in as many rows as you want to.

Number of sides (S)	Number of triangles (S − 2)	T × 180°
4	2	360°
5	3	

You have been looking at angle sums of regular polygons so far. The same results are true for
irregular polygons. Draw a square (a regular shape) and some more quadrilaterals.
(A quadrilateral is any four-sided shape.) If you join up all the sides from one vertex of the
quadrilateral, you will still make two triangles and the angle sum will remain the same.
Try it out for other polygons, if you are still not convinced.

Some common quadrilaterals

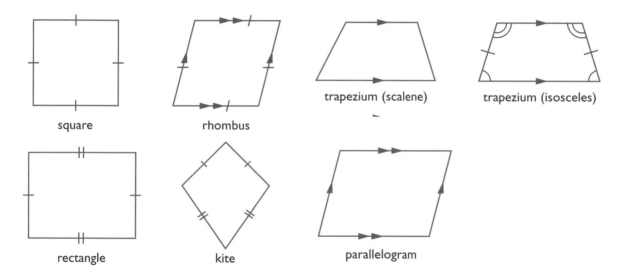

square rhombus trapezium (scalene) trapezium (isosceles)

rectangle kite parallelogram

Exercise 2

Find the sum of the interior angles of shapes with the following numbers of sides.

1 5
2 8
3 7
4 20

Tactics

Remember! A rhombus is like a
square that has been pushed out
of shape, and a parallelogram is
like a rectangle that has been
pushed out of shape. A kite has
two pairs of adjacent equal sides.
A trapezium has one pair of
unequal, parallel sides.

Constructions

How to use a protractor

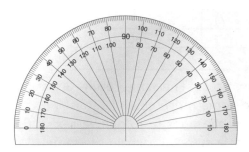
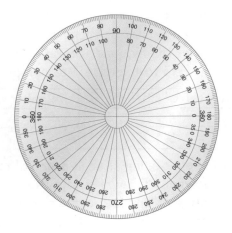

You can choose whether to use a 180° or 360° protractor. They both work in the same way, although you need a little more thought when you are using a 180° one.

- Put your protractor over the angle which you are measuring, so that the central cross of the protractor is over the point of the angle and the base line of the protractor is over one of the lines of the angle.
- The other line of the angle will point to two numbers on the scale around the edge of the protractor. Sometimes it is obvious which value is required, but if in doubt, look at the position of the zero on the protractor which is on the base line of the angle. If the zero is on the outside, read along the outside scale, and if it is on the inside, read along the inside scale.

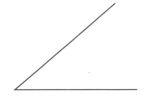
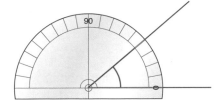
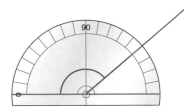

Exercise 1

Measure these angles. Turn the page round if it helps.
Give each answer to the nearest degree.

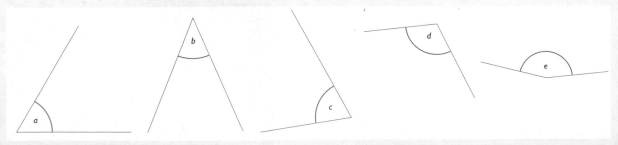

How to use a ruler and protractor to draw shapes

Example
Each interior angle of a regular hexagon is 120°. Use a ruler and protractor to draw a regular hexagon with each side 5 cm.

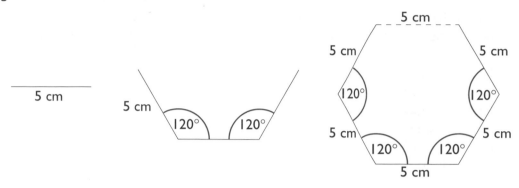

Example
Draw triangle WXY so that XY is 10 cm long, ∠WXY is a right angle and ∠WYX = 60°.
Measure WX and WY.

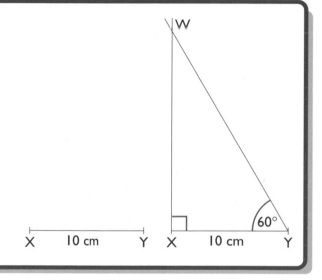

Exercise 2

1 Use a ruler and protractor to construct triangle ABC, so that AB = 10 cm, ∠BAC = 70° and ∠CBA = 55°.
2 Measure the length AC.
3 What do you notice about it?
4 What kind of a triangle is triangle ABC?

Tactics
The lines that you draw are *construction lines*.
Always leave them on to show your working.

Two-dimensional shapes

Tessellating shapes

When polygons can be put together, with no gaps between them, they tessellate. Not all polygons tessellate. Their interior angles must be factors of 360° for them to fit together around a point.

Squares tessellate, and so do any triangles, parallelograms (including rhombuses), kites and trapezia. You can check this for yourself in the exercise below.

Use triangles, squares, hexagons and octagons to make tessellating patterns.

Try using different combinations of shapes. How many different patterns can you make?

Draw your own basic shapes, or trace the ones on this page and the next on to card and cut them out to use as templates.

Exercise 1

1 The first diagram shows part of a tessellation of squares and regular octagons. Work out the size of the interior angle of a regular octagon. Explain your answer.
2 Why do octagons tessellate with squares?
3 The second diagram shows part of a tessellation of regular hexagons. Work out the size of an interior angle of a regular hexagon.
4 Which of the following shapes will tessellate?
   a equilateral triangles   b squares   c hexagons
   d pentagons   e rectangles

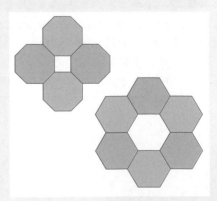

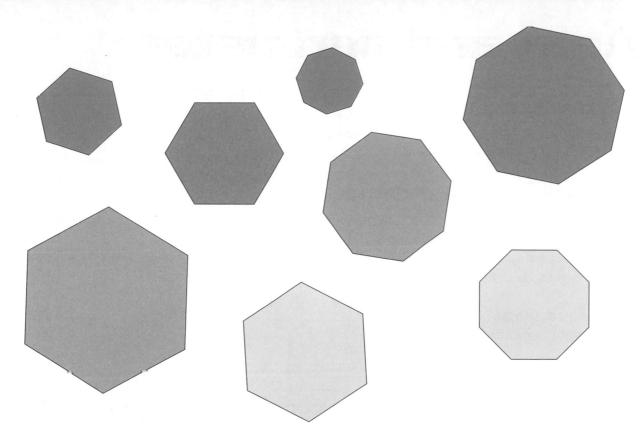

Congruent shapes

Shapes that are exactly the same as each other, in shape and in size, are congruent. One could be laid over the other exactly.

Because congruent shapes are identical, their areas will be identical. However, not all shapes with the same area are congruent. A square with sides 4 cm would have the same area as a rectangle with sides 8 cm and 2 cm, but the shapes are not congruent.

Exercise 2

Complete the following sentences.

1 Shape A is congruent to shape .... .
2 Shape B is congruent to shape .... .
3 Shape C is congruent to shape .... .
4 Shape D is congruent to shape .... .
5 Shape E is congruent to shape .... .
6 Shape F is congruent to shape .... .

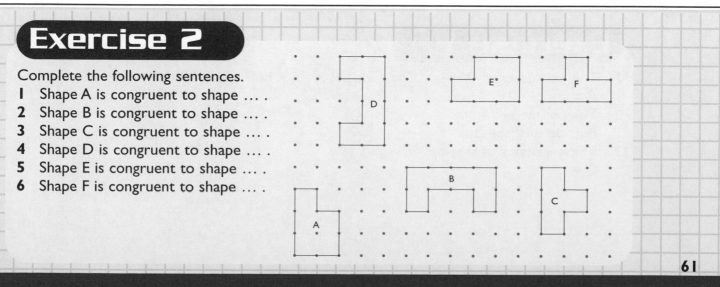

Area and perimeter

Understanding the jargon

Area the flat space occupied by a shape, or inside it
Perimeter the distance all round a shape

Measuring area and perimeter

Area is usually measured in square centimetres (cm^2), square metres (m^2), or square kilometres (km^2). To find area of squares, rectangles and triangles, use the formulae.
Perimeter is usually measured in millimetres (mm), centimetres (cm), metres (m) or kilometres (km). To find the perimeter, add the lengths of all the sides.

Area of a rectangle
area = length × width

Area of a triangle

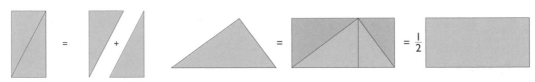

area = $\frac{1}{2}$ × base length × height or area

  = $\frac{\text{base length} \times \text{height}}{2}$

Exercise 1

1   The perimeter of shape
    A =
2   The perimeter of the
    outside of shape B =
3   The perimeter of shape
    C =

These shapes are not drawn accurately.

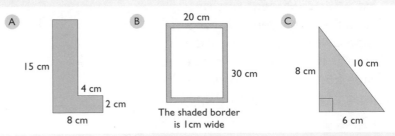

Be careful with units. 'Area is squarea' – if the perimeter is measured in
centimetres, the area will be in square centimetres (cm^2).

Compound shapes

It is easy to find the area of a shape that is made up of other shapes if you split it up, and then add together all the pieces.
The diagrams are not accurately drawn, so you cannot measure them to find the area.

Example

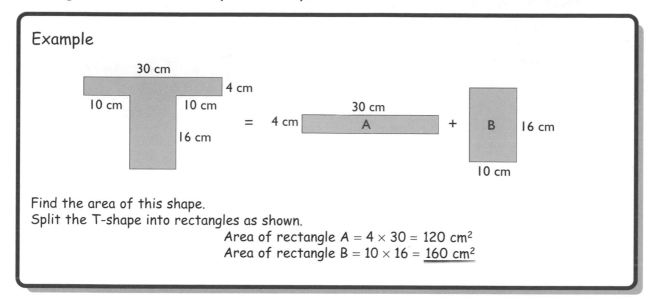

Find the area of this shape.
Split the T-shape into rectangles as shown.

$$\text{Area of rectangle A} = 4 \times 30 = 120 \text{ cm}^2$$
$$\text{Area of rectangle B} = 10 \times 16 = \underline{160 \text{ cm}^2}$$

Sometimes it is easier to subtract areas.

Example

The diagram represents a lawn 15 m by 10 m, with a pond 4 m square in it.
Find the area of the lawn.

$$\text{The total area} = 15 \times 10 \text{ m}^2 = 150 \text{ m}^2$$
$$\text{The area of the pond} = 4 \times 4 \text{ m}^2 = \underline{16 \text{ m}^2}$$
$$\text{The area of the lawn} = 134 \text{ m}^2$$

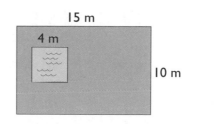

Exercise 2

1 The area of shape A =
2 The area of the shaded part of shape B =
3 The area of shape C =

These shapes are not drawn accurately.

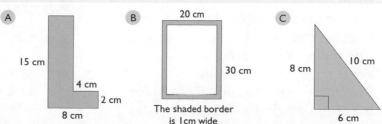

The shaded border is 1cm wide

Views

Understanding the jargon

Cube a 3D shape with identical square faces
Cuboid a 3D shape with rectangular faces,
opposite faces are equal

Nets

A hollow 3D shape, such as a cube or
cuboid, cut along its edges, opened out
and laid flat, forms a net.
There is often more than one way to draw a net.
Here are two possible nets for the
cuboid in the diagram above.

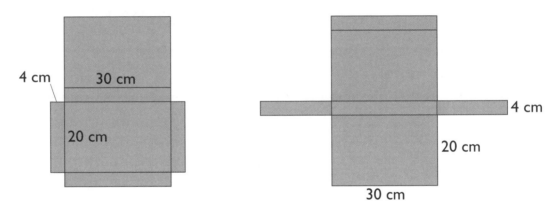

Be careful when drawing nets.
Sometimes they are closed (have lids) and sometimes they are open (without lids).

Surface area

The area of the net of a 3D shape is the same as the surface area of the shape.

Exercise 1

The diagram shows a model made with unit
   cubes.
1 How many unit cubes would you need
   to make this model?
2 Find the area of face A.
3 What is the area of face B?
4 Sketch the side elevation (Face A) for
   the shape. Mark the lengths of
   each side.

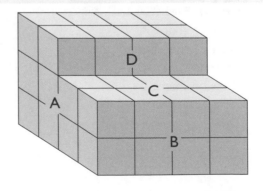

Example

Shape D is a cube. All sides are the same length.
Shape E is a cuboid. Opposite sides are the same length.
The sides in shape D are 5 cm long.
The sides in shape E are 5 cm, 6 cm and 8 cm long.
Draw nets and find the surface areas of each.

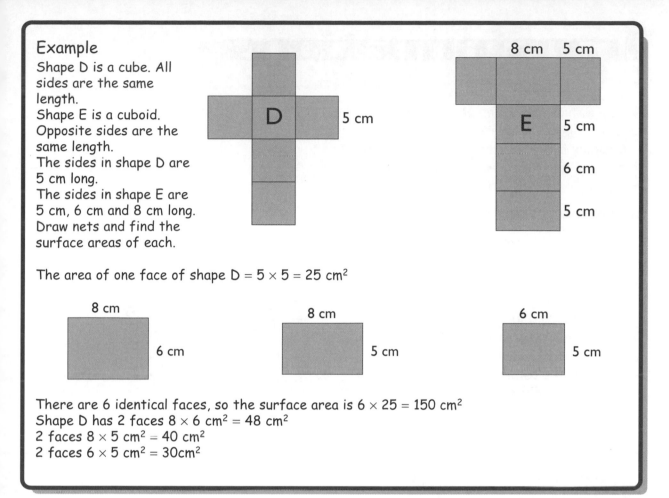

The area of one face of shape D = $5 \times 5 = 25$ cm²

There are 6 identical faces, so the surface area is $6 \times 25 = 150$ cm²
Shape D has 2 faces 8×6 cm² = 48 cm²
2 faces 8×5 cm² = 40 cm²
2 faces 6×5 cm² = 30cm²

Plan and elevation

The plan view is the view looking down on an object.
The front elevation is the view from the front of an object.
The side view is the view from the side of an object.

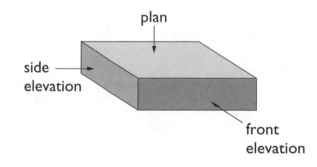

Exercise 2

These are the plan (top view), the side elevation (view from the side) and the front elevation (view from the front) of Wayne's hifi unit. Write down which is which.

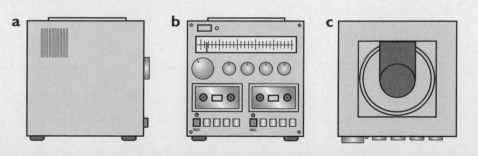

a

b

c

Transformations

Moving a shape from one place to another, or making it bigger or smaller is called transforming or mapping it. The original shape is called the object. The new shape is called the image. The change is called a transformation.

Symmetry and reflection

If a shape has symmetry, it can be folded along a line and one half will fit exactly over the other. In a reflection, each point in the object is mapped to its corresponding point in the image by being reflected in a mirror line.
The diagram shows shapes and their images after reflection in various lines.
A mirror line is sometimes called a reflection line or an axis of symmetry.

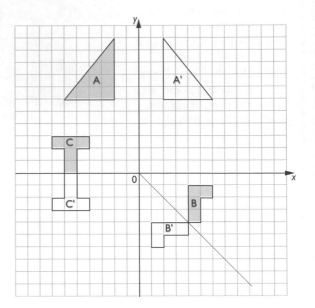

Exercise 1

Complete the reflections in these diagrams. Use any colour you like.

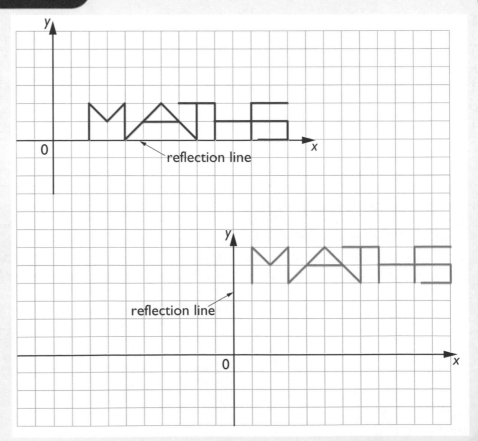

Key facts

* The object and its image are the same shape and size (congruent), although you would have to flip one of them over to make it fit on top of the other.
* The object and its image are the same distance from the mirror line.
* Points on the mirror line remain in the same position after a reflection.
* When a point in the object is labelled, for example, A, its image is usually labelled A′.
* Mirror lines can be vertical, horizontal or sloping.

Translations

When an object is translated, each point is mapped to its image by moving the same distance horizontally and the same distance vertically.

Key facts

* The object and its image are congruent.
* Both the object and its image are facing the same way.
* Translations are described using two instructions – movement parallel to the x-axis and movement parallel to the y-axis. In other words, always describe the movement across before the movement up or down.

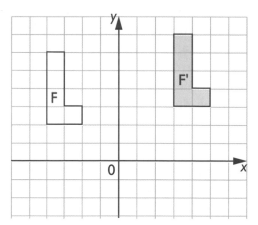

From F to F′ is forward 7, up 1.
From F′ to F is back 7, down 1.

Exercise 2

J, K, L, M, N, O, P, Q, R, S, T, U, V, W, X, Y, Z

1 Which of these letters have exactly one axis of symmetry?
2 Which of these letters have exactly two axes of symmetry?
3 Which of these letters have more than two axes of symmetry?
4 Which of these letters have no axes of symmetry?

Exercise 3

1 Draw a triangle on squared paper. Translate every point on the triangle 3 units to the left and 4 units up.
  What translation would you use to move the image back to its original position?
2 A translation moves every point 4 units to the right and 6 units down.
  What translation would you use to move every point back to its starting position?

Tactics

You will often find it helpful to use tracing paper for work on transformations. Trace the object and move, twist or turn the tracing until it fits the image.

Rotations

In a rotation, the object turns through an angle, about a central point called the centre of rotation. If corresponding points in the object and the image are joined to the centre of rotation by straight lines, the angle between the lines is the same for every pair of points. This is the angle of rotation.

Key facts
- The object and its image are congruent (identical, the same shape and size).
- The centre of rotation can be inside or outside the shape and is the only that point remains in the same position after a rotation.
- The number of ways that you can rotate a shape around a point inside itself so that it still looks the same is called the order of rotation.
- When describing a rotation, state the centre of rotation, the angle of rotation and whether the rotation is clockwise or anti-clockwise.

It is often easier to find the centre of rotation of a shape by using tracing paper. After tracing the shape, put your pencil on the point where you think that the centre should be and swivel the tracing. If you are right, the shape should lie on its image.

Exercise 4

1 Rotate the flag F 90° clockwise around the origin, labelled O. Label the new flag F′.
2 Rotate F′ 90° clockwise around point O. Label the new flag F″.
3 How many degrees do you need to rotate F″ to return it to its original position?
4 Does it matter whether this last rotation is clockwise or anti-clockwise? Give a reason for your answer.

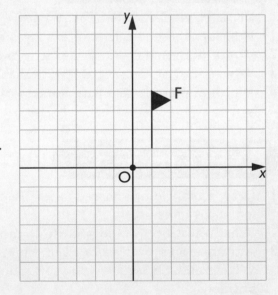

Combining transformations

Sometimes a shape can be mapped to its image by more than one transformation.
S can be mapped to S' and then S' can be mapped to S''.
S can also be mapped directly to S'' by reflection in the line $y = -x$.

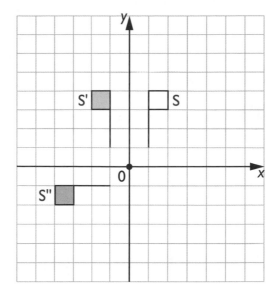

Exercise 5

1 Refer to the diagram above.
   a Shape S maps to S' by a ... .
   b Shape S' maps to S'' by a ... .
   c Shape S'' maps to S' by a ... .
   d Shape S' maps to S by a ... .
2 **a** What transformation maps T to T'?
   b What transformation maps T' to T''?
   c What transformation maps T'' to T'?
   d What transformation maps T' to T?
3 If you reflect a shape and then translate it, do you get the same result as if you reversed the order of operations?

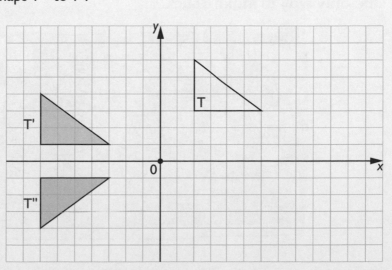

3

Things to do: sort out a revision plan

● Does this sound familiar?

- I can do maths in class, but I can't remember it when I do my homework

- I understand it when we do it, but I forget it by the time the next lesson comes round.

- I'm just getting the hang of it when we move on to something else.

- I haven't kept my old exercise books and I can't remember how to do things.

If you have said, 'That's me!' at least once, then you need this section!

Most people forget that they weren't born able to read and write. They had to learn how to do it, and it probably took a great deal of practice. However, once you can read and write, you don't even think about it. You just take it for granted.

● For most people, going over what they have learned until it is automatic is the only way to make it stick.

Organise your learning

Next time you have a test coming up, don't leave everything until the last moment. Tests usually involve learning lists of facts, or foreign vocabulary, and can be very worrying. Almost everybody has a problem, at some time, learning and remembering what seems like stacks of new material, but for some people it is a real problem.

- Start well in advance, so that you have time to keep going over what you have learned.

   Suppose you had to learn 20 French words for a vocabulary test. First, see if there are any that you already know, or can guess because they are like English words. Divide the total of the remainder by the number of days that you have to learn them, and, hopefully you won't have more than about four a day. Write them on sticky notes that you can attach to pieces of furniture so that you keep seeing them – the inside of a wardrobe door is often a good place – and make an extra copy to carry with you. Glance at it in any spare moments during the day.

- You could record yourself, or make notes on the computer, although you may find that you will have to learn special key combinations to cope with some of the symbols or accents used in other languages.

- On the next revision day, repeat the process for the new facts, but make sure that you go back over the material that you learned the day before. Keep repeating the pattern until the test and – who knows? – you'll probably pass with flying colours.

- Keep your completed exercise books in a safe place. At secondary school you will probably have end-of-year exams in most subjects, and it will be much easier to revise if you have your earlier work to jog your memory. You can adapt the ideas for revising for tests to exam revision too.

Averages and range

Understanding the jargon

Mode the most common value in a given set.

Modal group the range of values that occurs most often (has the highest frequency) in a set of grouped data, e.g. ages 5–9

Mean the sum of all the values in a set of data, divided by the number of values in the set

To find the mean, add up all the values in a set and divided by the number of values which you have.

Median the middle value when all the data values are arranged in order, smallest to largest or vice versa

Range the difference between the largest value and the smallest value in the data, for example, if the smallest value in the set is 7 and the largest is 12, the range is 5.

Examples

Say whether you would use the mean, the median or the mode to find out:

a how pupils travel to school

b whether boys or girls in a given year group get more pocket money

c people's favourite newspaper

d what percentage of trains run on time in a given week

e your average mark after a set of tests

f which size of sandal should a shop stock in order to maximise sales (sell most pairs).

For *a* and *c* you must choose the **mode**.

You should also choose the **mode** for *f*. It would be pointless to stock up on size $5\frac{1}{2}$ if most sales were sizes 5 and 6; the same argument goes for not using the mean.

For *b*, *d* or *e* you could choose the **mean** or the **median**, depending on your data.

Choosing between the mean or the median

The mean of the set of numbers 5, 7, 8, 9, 10 is 7.8 and the median is 8.

The mean of the set of numbers 5, 7, 8, 9, 350 is 75.8 and the median is 8.

If you have one or two values that are much bigger or smaller than the other values, it will greatly affect the mean, so it is more accurate to use the median.

Exercise 1

Find:

a the mode **b** the mean

c the median

for these sets of numbers.

1 4, 6, 11, 14, 1, 8, 6, 3, 10

2 2, 2.5, 1.5, 3.8, 1.5, 4.6

Tactics

When people talk about finding the average, they are usually referring to the mean, but there are different types of average, all with different uses. You will need to know about all three.

RED **Before you pick the median, remember to put the data in order, smallest to largest.** ALERT RED ALERT RE

Finding the modal group

> **Example**
> A teacher gave a class a maths problem, and noted how long the pupils took to solve it.
>
> | Time taken (seconds) | 10-14 | 15-19 | 20-24 | 25-29 | 30 or more |
> |---|---|---|---|---|---|
> | Number of pupils | 2 | 15 | 8 | 3 | 2 |
>
> The modal group is 15-19, because there are more pupils in that group than in any other.

Finding the mean

> **Example**
> Thirty pupils took part in a sponsored swim for charity. They collected these amounts.
>
> | Amount collected (£) | 5 | 6 | 7 | 8 | 9 | 10 |
> |---|---|---|---|---|---|---|
> | Number of students | 3 | 7 | 5 | 7 | 6 | 2 |
>
> a   How much money was collected?
> b   What was the mean amount collected per student?
> a   Three pupils each collected £5.00, so their total was 3 × £5.00 = £15.00.
>   Seven pupils each collected £6.00, so their total was £42.00 and so on . . .
>   3 × £5.00 + 7 × £6.00 + 5 × £7.00 + 7 × £8.00 + 6 × £9.00 + 2 × £10.00 = £222.00
> b   The mean amount = total collected ÷ number of students = £222.00 ÷ 30 = £7.40.

> **Examples**
> • The mean of the numbers on these cards is 6. Find the missing value.
>   Start by finding the total. This is the number of cards × the mean
>   value. 6 + 6 + 6 + 6 + 6 = 5 × 6 = 30
>   Then 8 + 3 + 5 + 1 + ? = 30 ⇒ The missing value is 30 − 7 = 13.
>
> | 8 | 3 | 5 | 1 | |
>
> • The mean of the numbers on these five cards is 8 and they have
>   a range of 6. Find the missing values.
>   Start by finding the total. 5 × 8 = 40
>   Values on the three cards = 24. So the total value of the missing cards = 40 − 24 = 16.
>   As the range is 6, one value will be 3 more than the mean and one will be 3 less than the
>   mean. The missing numbers are 5 and 11.
>
> | 8 | 8 | 8 | | |

Exercise 2

Find:
a   the mean   b   the median
c   the mode   d   the range
for this set of numbers.
8, 6, 10, 4, 12, 7, 8, 15, 11

Tactics

Remember you have first to
multiply to find the total.
It may help to remember 'In
the mean time, times for the
total'.

The mode is the value that occurs most often,
not the number of people who chose it – and
there can be more than one mode!

ERT   ALERT RED ALERT

Samples and surveys

Understanding the jargon

Survey When you are doing research involving a group of people, you will have to carry out a survey. This often involves asking them questions, or getting them to fill in a questionnaire.

Sample As there are often too many people involved to ask absolutely everybody, we usually pick a group from all those who could be chosen. For instance, if you wanted to find out Year 7 pupils' opinions on school dinners, you might give a questionnaire to 20 or so students in each form.

Random In a random sample, everyone has the same chance of being chosen. In the above example, for instance, you might pick names out of a hat containing the names of all the Year 7 students.

Asking questions

You have to take care that people cannot be in more than one category simultaneously.

> **Examples**
>
> What is wrong with this range of ages?
>
> Age (years)   5-10   10-15   15-20   20+
>
> People who are ten, fifteen or twenty years old are in two categories.
>
> A better classification would be
>
> Age (years)   5-9   10-14   15-19   20+

Exercise 1

1 The bar chart shows the results of a survey on wildlife seen in one week in people's gardens.

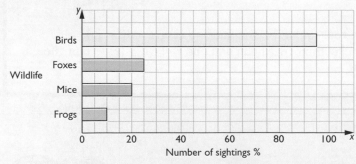

What percentage of sightings were there of:

a birds   **b** foxes
c frogs   **d** mice?

2 Use the grid below to draw a line graph to show this information. The entry for mice has been done for you.

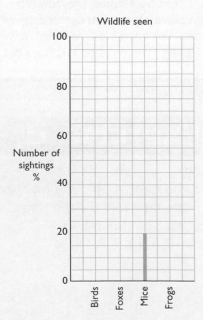

74

Collecting data

Suppose you are carrying out a survey into the amount of time people spent on homework on any given evening. You might make a list similar to the one below. The list of information obtained from the sample is called a **data information sheet**.

To make it easier to read, you can group the answers in fives as shown. This is tallying.

> ### Example
> A group of 28 pupils were asked how long they spent on homework one evening. Which time span is the modal group?
> *How much time did you spend doing homework last night?*
> Less than 1 hour   ///
> Between 1 and 2 hours   //// //// //// ///
> More than 2 hours   //// //
> The mode, which is the most commonly occurring group was 'Between 1 and 2 hours'.

Displaying data

Results of surveys may be displayed in:
- bar charts
- line graphs
- pictograms
- pie charts.

Exercise 2

1 The pictogram shows the numbers of packets of crisps sold to Year 7 students each day for a week.

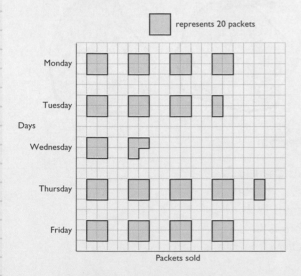

represents 20 packets

a On which day were most crisps sold?
b On which two days were the some number of crisps sold?
c How many more crisps were sold on Thursday than on Tuesday?

d On one day that week there was a school trip for some Year 7 members. Which day do you think was the day of the trip?

2 The pie chart shows the results of a survey on class 7G's favourite colours. How many degrees do you need to draw for each group?

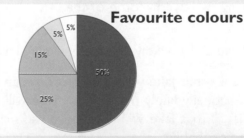

Favourite colours

Tactics

In pictograms, choose symbols that can easily be divided to show the data.

75

Probability

Use Exercise 2, questions 1 and 2, to check your knowledge of basic number work, before you go on. If you need help with any of these, look back to page 20.

Understanding the jargon

Event the action being measured, such as throwing dice, tossing a coin or choosing a card
Outcome a result of an event
Throwing a normal dice is an event that has six possible outcomes, whereas tossing a coin has two possible outcomes (excluding the rare chance that the coin lands and rests on its edge!).

Biased and unbiased outcomes

If all outcomes have an equal chance of occurring, they are unbiased. If not, one or more of the outcomes is biased.

Measuring probability

- Probability of outcomes is measured in fractions, decimals or percentages.
- For any event, the probabilities for all possible outcomes add up to 1.
- The probability of something not happening is 1 minus the probability of it happening.

Exercise 1

Josh and Jake are doing an experiment. Each has a bag with marbles. They take a marble out of their bags, note the colour and return the marble to the bag. After ten turns each, they compare results. Fill in the spaces. You will need to use the following words for some of the answers.

Josh's bag   Jake's bag

| impossible | unlikely | equally likely | likely | certain |

1 It is ... that Jake will draw more green marbles than Josh.
2 It is equally likely that Josh or Jake will take a ... marble.
3 It is ... that Jake will take more red marbles than Josh.
4 The probability that ... will take a green marble is 0.4.
5 The probability that Josh will take a red or yellow marble is ... .

The probability line

You may have to use a probability line to answer a probability question.

Examples

Write letters on the line as shown to illustrate the various probabilities.

a If today is Tuesday, tomorrow will be Wednesday.

b If I toss a coin I will throw a head.

c Tomorrow the sun will rise in the west in England.

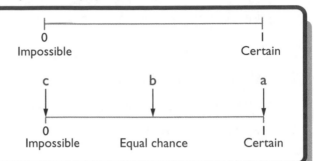

Examples

The letters of the word ELEPHANT are written separately on cards and placed in a box. Write, as a fraction, the probability of picking out:

a the letter T   *b* the letter E   *c* a vowel   *d* a consonant (not a vowel).

Write each fraction in its lowest terms.

a $\frac{1}{8}$ *b* $\frac{2}{8} = \frac{1}{4}$ *c* $\frac{3}{8}$ *d* $\frac{5}{8}$

Exercise 2

1 **a** $\frac{3}{5} + \frac{1}{5}$ **b** $1 - 0.65$ **c** $0.4 + 0.3$ **d** $35\% + 65\%$ **e** $1 - \frac{3}{8}$

2 **a** Change $\frac{3}{8}$ to a decimal.   **b** Change 0.38 to a percentage.

3 **a** List all the possible outcomes when a coin is tossed twice.

   b If you toss a coin twice, what is the probability of getting two tails?

   c If you toss a coin twice, what is the probability of getting at least one head?

   d If you toss a coin twice, what is the probability that you will get one head and one tail?

Exercise 3

A group of students carried out a survey to find out Year 7's favourite sport.

Answer these questions and write your answers as decimals.

1 What is the probability that cycling is the favourite sport of one of these students chosen at random?

2 What is the probability that the favourite sport of one student chosen at random is martial arts or swimming?

3 What is the probability that a student chosen at random will not choose football?

Favourite sport	No. of students
Cycling	25
Football	72
Hockey	34
Martial arts	14
Swimming	36
Tennis	19

Tactics

If your answer for a probability is negative or greater than 1 it is wrong, and that is a certainty!

The total probability for all the possible outcomes is always exactly 1.

TEST PAPER 1

Mental arithmetic test

If possible, ask someone else to read this test aloud for you. Write your answers down as quickly as you can.

1   Write the number ten thousand and nine, in figures.

2   Add one hundred and ninety-nine to four hundred and twenty-seven.

3   What is seven multiplied by eight?

4   Write the number six and a half million in figures.

5   The area of a square is 36 cm². What is its perimeter?

6   There are twelve chocolates and eight toffees in a box. I choose one sweet at random. What is the probability that I choose a chocolate?

7   Find the value of 2*a* + 10 when *a* is equal to 4.5.

8   What is half of six and a quarter?

9   Which integer is nearest to the square root of 131?

10   Name a quadrilateral which always has just one axis of symmetry.

11   Five numbers have a mean of six. What is their total?

12   Three consecutive numbers have a total of 27. What is the largest of these numbers?

13   A right-angled triangle has a base of four centimetres and a vertical height of six centimetres. What is its area?

14   What is the next number in the sequence 1, 4, 7, 10, … ?

15   What is three-quarters written as a percentage?

16   How many sweets, at twenty pence each, could you buy for one pound and sixty pence?

17   What is the order of symmetry of a square?

18   If the probability of an event happening is three-fifths, what is the probability of it not happening?

19   The largest angle in an isosceles triangle is 100 degrees. What is the size of each of the other angles?

20   Write six hundred and thirty-five centimetres in metres.

21   Five miles are approximately equal to eight kilometres. How many miles are approximately equal to twelve kilometres?

22   A boy is *n* years old and his sister is 6 years older than he is. How many years old is she in terms of *n*?

23   Two people share £24.00 in the ratio 3 : 1. What is the smaller share?

24   What is 6.4 divided by 100?

25   What must you add to negative three to make seven?

Responses

1 _____

2 _____

3 _____

4 _____

5 _____

6 _____

7 _____

8 _____

9 _____

10 _____

11 _____

12 _____

13 _____

14 _____

15 _____

16 _____

17 _____

18 _____

19 _____

20 _____

21 _____

22 _____

23 _____

24 _____

25 _____

TEST PAPER 2

Time allowed: 1 hour   Do not use a calculator for this paper.

1 Fill in the gaps.

    a To change centimetres to metres, ... centimetres by ....

    b To change centimetres to millimetres, ... centimetres by ....

    c To change tonnes to kilograms, ... tonnes by ....

    d To change grams to kilograms, ... grams by ....

2 Amber is drawing patterns. The rule for Amber's pattern is $t = 2n + 4$.

    a Draw the next pattern which she will make.

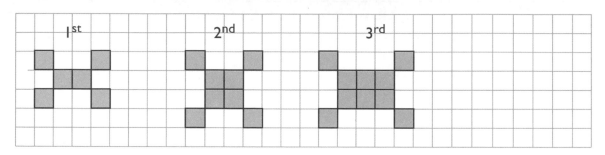

    b How many squares will she draw for pattern number 15?

    _____

3 Katie is painting some scenery for a school play. The colour she needs is
  made by mixing 3 parts of red paint with 2 parts of green and 1 of blue.

    a Write this as a ratio red : green : blue.

    _____

    b If she needs 18 litres of this paint altogether, how much of each colour

       does she need?

    _____

    c If she only has $1\frac{1}{2}$ litres of blue paint, but plenty of red and green, what is

       the maximum amount of the colour which she could make?

    _____

    d What fraction of the amount is she still short?

    _____

4 On the diagram, draw the reflection of the shape
  in the mirror line provided.

  What is the name of the new shape?

    _____

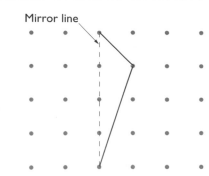

Mirror line

5 View A shows a model made with 6 cubes. View B shows the same model with one cube missing. Complete the drawing from view B.

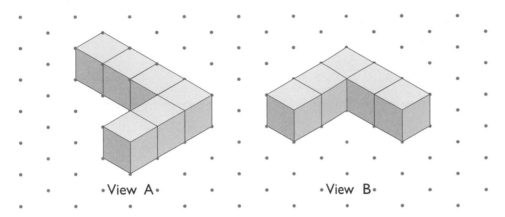

•View A• •View B•

6 a Fill in the next number in the sequence. 1, 4, 9, 16, ...

b These numbers have a special name. What is it?

7 a The mean of these six cards is 20. What is the total score of the six cards?

20 20 20 20

b The range of the six cards is eight. What are the values on the missing two cards?

8 This game is played with a pack of 30 cards.
Twenty have a square on them, and 10 have a star.
Each player takes it in turns to draw a card.

a Is the first player more likely to draw a card with a square or a star on it?

b Five cards have been drawn, each with a square. Paul says that as the first five cards have had squares, the next card is more likely to have a star. Explain why Paul is wrong.

c Jane says that as each card has either a square or a star, there is an equal chance of the next card having either a square or a star. Explain why Jane is wrong.

TEST PAPER 2

Form 7J found these results.

The remaining students cycled.
What percentage of students cycled?

✎ _____

Car	50%
Walk	20%
Bus	17%
Train	3%

10 The temperature at midnight in Manchester one night in January was 3 °C.
Two hours later it had fallen by five degrees.

   a What was the temperature then?

   ✎ _____

By noon the next day it had risen by seven degrees.

   b What was the temperature at noon on that day?

   ✎ _____

11 A school coach trip is planned for 415 members of Year 7 including some staff. Assume each coach carries 50 passengers.

   a Make a rough calculation to estimate the number of coaches needed.

   ✎ _____

   b If each coach can carry 56 people, how many coaches will be needed?

   ✎ _____

12 This triangle is not drawn to scale.
Work out the answers to these questions.

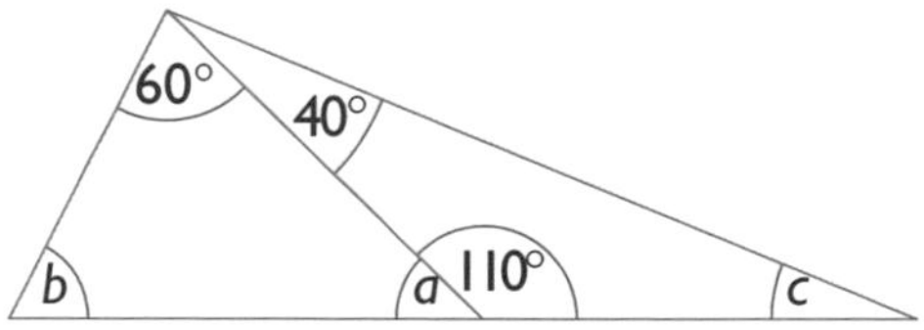

   a *a* is ...... degrees because
   ....

   b *b* is ...... degrees because
   ....

   c *c* is ...... degrees because ....

13 Fill in the spaces.

   a Angle ...... and angle ...... are acute angles.

   b Angle ...... and angle ...... are obtuse angles.

   c Angle ...... and angle ...... are reflex angles.

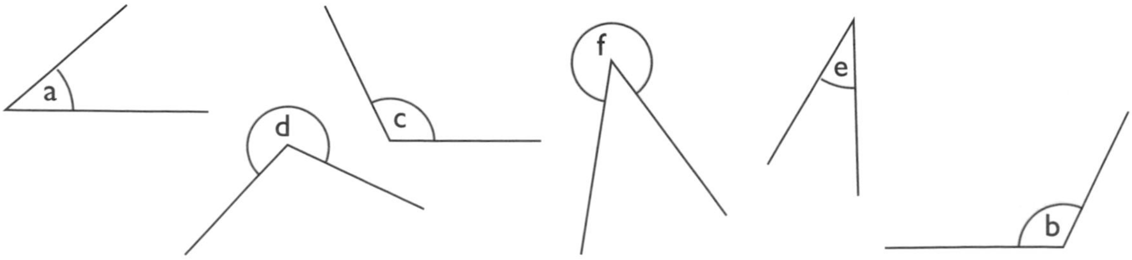

82

14 David is playing a game. Each player is dealt four cards and has to make a number according to a rule.

    a The rule in this round is: *Make the largest number you can.*

      What number should David make?

      _____

    b In the next round, the rule is: Make a number that divides by 5.

      What number could David make?

      _____

15 A café sells beefburgers, cheeseburgers and veggieburgers with small or large chips. Fill in the boxes below to show the number of different combinations which you could buy. You may not need to use all the lines.
One combination has been done for you.

Burgers	Chips
cheese	small

16 The area of a square is 36 cm².

    a How long is each side of the square?

      _____

    b What is its perimeter?

      _____

    c How many of these squares could you fit into a rectangle 24 cm wide and 30 cm long?

      _____

TEST PAPER 3

Time allowed: 1 hour   You may use a calculator for this paper.

1 a Put in $+, -, \times$ or $\div$ to complete this calculation.

    16 ...... 2 ...... 23 = 31

b Put brackets in these calculations to make them correct.

  i $5 + 7 \times 2 = 24$ **ii** $20 - 5 \div 2 + 3 = 3$

_____   _____

c Work out the answers to $5 + 7 \times 2$ and $20 - 5 \div 2 + 3$ (without brackets).

_____

2 Write 'True' or 'False' after each statement.

a $n + n + n = 3n$ **b** $n \times n = n^2$ **c** $2n^2 = 2 \times n \times n$

_____   _____   _____

d $(2n)^2 = 2n \times 2n = 4n^2$ **e** $a \div b = \dfrac{a}{b}$ **f** $ab = a \times b$

_____   _____   _____

3

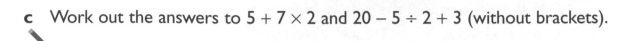

For this function machine:

a when the input is 6, the output is _____

_____

b when the input is 0.7, the output is _____ .

_____

4

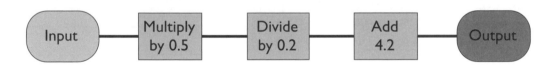

For this function machine:

a when the output is 12 the input is _____

_____

b when the output is 1.5, the input is _____ .

_____

5 Use a calculator to work these out, giving each answer correct to two decimal places.

    a 23.75×2.87 **b** $168.6 \div 0.07$ **c** 23.46×35.78

    ✎ _____   ✎ _____   ✎ _____

6 **a** Using AB as a base line, draw $\angle A = 70°$ and $\angle B = 35°$.

    ✎ Extend the sides and label the point where they cross C.

              A ──────────────────── B

   b Without measuring, work out the size of $\angle ACB$. Show your working.

    ✎ _____

7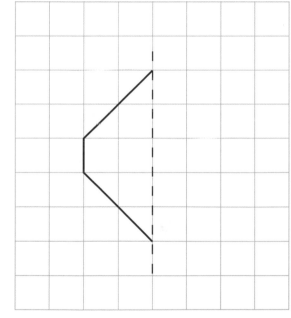

   a Complete the diagram, using the dotted line as an axis (line) of symmetry.

   b What is the name of the complete shape?

    ✎ _____

   c What is the area of one small square?

    ✎ _____

   d What is the area of the complete shape?

    ✎ _____

8 Suppose today is Monday. On the number line below, write:

    ✎ _____

  a A to show the probability that tomorrow will be Sunday

  b B to show the probability that tomorrow will be Tuesday.

                       ┌─────────────────────┐
                       0   0.5   1

9 The graph shows Jonathan's journey, when he walked from his house to the shop and back home again.

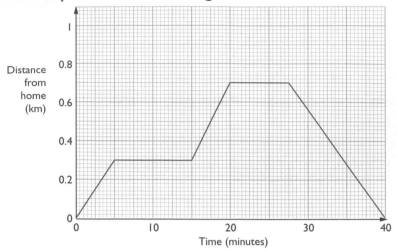

a How far is it from Jonathan's house to the shop?

_____

On the way, he stopped to talk to a friend.

b How far had he gone when he met his friend?

_____

c How long did he stop and talk?

_____

d How long did it take him to get to the shop after leaving his friend?

_____

e How long was he in the shop?

_____

f How long did it take him to get home after leaving the shop?

_____

g How far did he walk altogether?

_____

10 These amounts of money were collected for charity by a group of students.

Amount	£5.00	£5.50	£6.00	£6.50	£7.00	£7.50	£8.00
Number of students	3	7	8	2	5	4	1

a What was the total amount collected by the group?

_____

b What was the mean amount of money collected by the students?

_____

c What was the modal amount collected?

_____

11 a Six friends ordered a set meal at a restaurant. The bill came to £93.00. How much should each have paid?

b They decided to add a tip of 10%. How much extra did they pay?

c How much would the meal have cost, without the tip, for five friends?

12 From a packet of seeds, 25% of the flowers were red, 16% were white, 5% were pink and the rest were yellow.

a What percentage were yellow?

b Sunita has been told to display this information on a pie chart. What angle should she make the section that represents the red flowers?

13 On an activity holiday, a group split up to go swimming or rock climbing in the ratio 7 : 3.

If 12 students chose rock climbing, how many went swimming?

14 In a game, two spinners as shown are spun, and the scores are added together. List all the possible combinations.

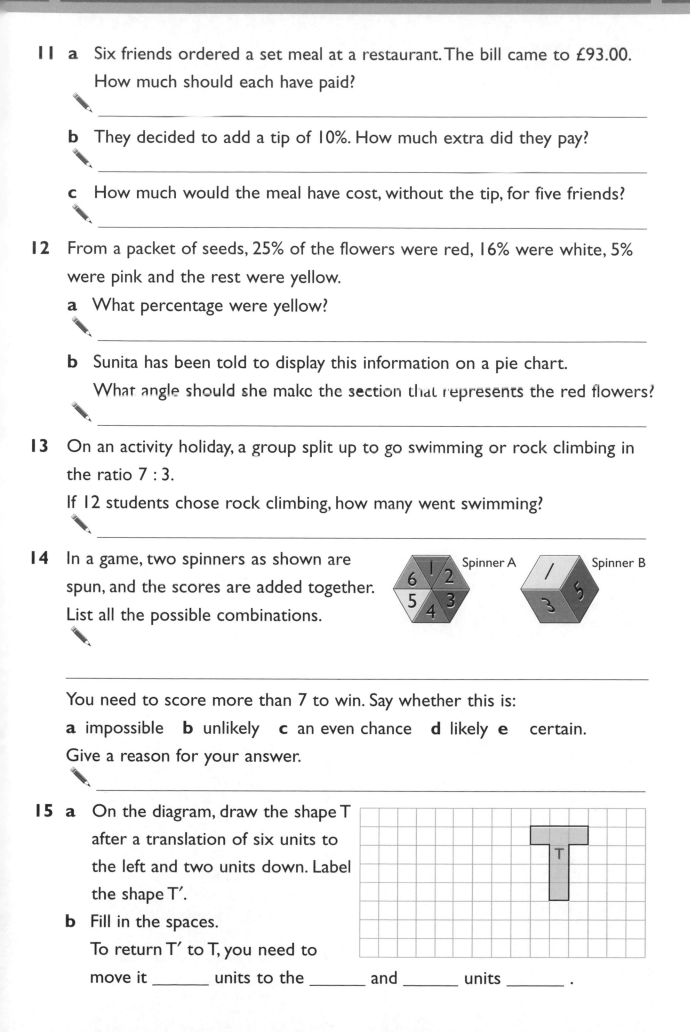

Spinner A

Spinner B

You need to score more than 7 to win. Say whether this is:

a impossible   **b** unlikely   **c** an even chance   **d** likely   **e** certain.

Give a reason for your answer.

15 a On the diagram, draw the shape T after a translation of six units to the left and two units down. Label the shape T′.

b Fill in the spaces.

To return T′ to T, you need to move it _____ units to the _____ and _____ units _____ .

ANSWERS

Answers to exercises

Number and algebra

Unit 1 The number system

Exercise 1 (page 8)

1 2301 2 30 018 3 2 105 009

Exercise 2 (page 9)

1 four million, six hundred thousand and thirty-four

2 two million, nineteen thousand and three

3 six million, four thousand and eighty

Exercise 3 (page 10)

1 **a** 75 000 **b** 56 000 **c** 2 300 000

2 **a** 340 **b** 10 000

Exercise 4 (page 10)

1 1920 2 2880 3 920

4 1020 5 2030

Exercise 5 (page 11)

1 **a** 2379 **b** 9732

2 **a** 0.01 **b** 0.19 **c** 0.019

3 **a** 34 286

   b thirty-four thousand, two hundred and eighty-six

   c **i** 342.86 **ii** 3.4286

Unit 2 Using decimals

Exercise 1 (page 12)

1 **a** 2.523 **b** 17.24 **c** 1.001

2 **a** 0.002, 0.031, 0.14, 0.3, 1.006

   b 0.002, 0.34, 1.95, 3.01

Exercise 2 (page 12)

1 2592 2 705 3 49.2

4 123.2 5 0.6

Exercise 3 (page 13)

1 439.5 2 1909.6 3 1044

4 351 5 30.42

Exercise 4 (page 13)

1 4.5 2 0.45 3 15

4 1.5 5 $24 \times 0.1 = 24 \div 10$

Unit 3 Types of number

Exercise 1 (page 14)

1 two from:

   a 1, 2, 4, 8   **b** 1, 2, 3, 4, 6, 12

   c 1, 13   **d** 1, 19

2 **a** 4, 8, 12, 16   **b** 5, 10, 15, 20

   c 6, 12, 18, 24   **d** 9, 18, 27, 36

3 2, 3, 5, 7, 11

Exercise 2 (page 14)

1 **a** 3, 5 **b** 2, 3, 5 **c** 2, 3

2 125

3 6

Exercise 3 (page 15)

1 **a** $2^5 \times 3^2$ **b** 2×5^3

2 **a** 504 **b** 675

Exercise 4 (page 16)

1 −8, −6, 1, 2, 3, 5

2 **a** 2 **b** −3 **c** 1

3 7, 5, 3, 1, −1, −3, −5, −7, −9

4 −9, −6, −3, 0, 3, 6, 9

5 −9, −3, 3

Exercise 5 (page 17)

1 5 2 −2 3 −10

4 $(5 - (-3) = 5 + 3 = 8)$

5 −7

6 $((-1) - (-3) = -1 + 3 = 2)$

Unit 4 Rounding and estimating

Exercise 1 (page 18)

1 **a** 23.46 **b** 16.08 **c** 8.70

2 **a** 6.1 **b** 35.0 **c** 23.1

3 **a** £23.15 **b** £0.67 **c** £75.80

   d £10.60 **e** £3.42 **f** £2.00

   g £1.05 **h** £0.15

4 **a** £4.62 **b** 304p

Exercise 2 (page 19)

These are suggested answers. You may have slightly different answers if you have rounded differently. There are no hard and fast rules.

1 $60 \times 4 = 240$ 2 $25 \times 4 = 100$

3 $500 \div 10 = 50$

4 £83.00 − £20.00 = £63.00

5 £150.00 + £200.00 = £350.00

Exercise 3 (page 19)

1 15 2 14.5 3 10.65 4 5.35

Unit 5 Decimals, percentages and fractions

Exercise 1 (page 20)

1 **a** 45% **b** 72% **c** 7%

   d 46% **e** 58% **f** 7%

2 **a** 0.43 **b** 0.28 **c** 0.25

   d 0.06 **e** 0.09 **f** 0.05

Exercise 2 (page 20)

1 5.4 2 5.6 3 35 4 12

Exercise 3 (page 21)

1 $\frac{3}{4} = \frac{6}{8} = \frac{12}{16}$ 2 $\frac{3}{5} = \frac{9}{15} = \frac{27}{45}$

3 $\frac{2}{3} = \frac{4}{6} = \frac{16}{24}$ 4 $\frac{20}{50} = \frac{2}{5}$ 5 $\frac{24}{40} = \frac{12}{20} = \frac{6}{10} = \frac{3}{5}$

Exercise 4 (page 22)

1 11 and 72 2 467, 310, 973

3 534, 411, 942

Exercise 5 (page 22)

1 **a** $\frac{2}{3}$ **b** $\frac{3}{5}$ **c** $\frac{3}{4}$ **d** $\frac{4}{5}$ **e** $\frac{2}{5}$ 2 $\frac{6}{9}$

Exercise 6 (page 23)

1 $2\frac{2}{5}$ 2 $9\frac{1}{2}$ 3 $4\frac{1}{2}$ 4 $8\frac{2}{3}$ 5 $2\frac{1}{2}$

Exercise 7 (page 23)

1 **a** $\frac{11}{2}$ **b** $\frac{11}{4}$ **c** $\frac{17}{4}$ **d** $\frac{21}{2}$ **e** $\frac{51}{4}$

2 $\frac{6}{9}$

Exercise 8 (page 24)

1 $£60.00 \div 4 \times 3 = £45.00$

2 $120 \div 8 \times 3 = 45$ potatoes

3 $\frac{1}{4}$

4 $\frac{1}{2}$ of 168 = 84 and $\frac{3}{4}$ of 108 = $108 \div 4 \times 3 = 81$ so $\frac{1}{2}$ of 168 is greater by 3.

ANSWERS

Exercise 9 (page 24)

1 $\frac{1}{10}$ **2** $\frac{1}{2}$ **3** $\frac{1}{4}$ **4** $\frac{3}{4}$ **5** $\frac{4}{25}$ **6** $\frac{5}{1000} = \frac{1}{200}$

Exercise 10 (page 25)

1 0.625 **2** 0.3 **3** 0.4 **4** 0.8 **5** 0.375

Exercise 11 (page 25)

1 0.67 **2** 0.27 **3** 0.56
4 0.43 **5** 0.44

Exercise 12 (page 25)

1 6% **2** 6.25 **3** 70%

Exercise 13 (page 26)

1 **a** $\frac{3}{8} = 0.375 = 37.5\%$

 b $\frac{7}{8} = 0.875 = 87.5\%$

 c $\frac{5}{8} = 0.625 = 62.5\%$

2 **a** $50\% = 0.5 = \frac{1}{2}$

 b $33\frac{1}{3}\% = 0.33 = \frac{1}{3}$ **c** $5\% = 0.05 = \frac{1}{20}$

3 **a** $0.1 = 10\% = \frac{1}{10}$ **b** $0.05 = 5\% = \frac{1}{20}$

 c $0.75 = 75\% = \frac{3}{4}$

Exercise 14 (page 27)

1 50% is red. 50% is blue.
2 70% is red. 30% is blue.
3 37.5% is red. 62.5% is blue.
4 40% is red. 60% is blue.

Unit 6 Using a scientific calculator

Exercise 1 (page 28)

1 479.74 **2** 1424.97 **3** 86.72 **4** 3050.57

Exercise 2 (page 29)

1 $3^3 \times 2^3 = 27 \times 8 = 216$
2 $5^8 = 390\,625, 8^5 = 32\,768$ so 5^8 is bigger.

Unit 7 Shortcuts and easy methods

Exercise 1 (page 30)

1 £20.94 **2** 600 **3** £2.00 **4** £53.94

Exercise 2 (page 31)

1 **a** £24.00 **b** £18.00 **c** 697 **d** 299
2 24 postcards

Unit 8 Proportion

Exercise 1 (page 32)

1 **a** $\frac{1}{4}$ **b** $\frac{3}{4}$ **c** 75% **d** 25%
 e 24 pupils **f** 8 pupils
2 **a** 250 ml **b** 750 ml **c** 625 ml

Exercise 2 (page 32)

1 **a** 20 toffees **b** 15 chocolates
 c 5 jellies
2 **a** 50% **b** 50%
3 **a** jellies **b** chocolates

Exercise 3 (page 33)

1 25% **2** $\frac{1}{2}$ **3** 75% **4** $\frac{7}{8}$ **5** $\frac{3}{8}$

Exercise 4 (page 33)

1 $\frac{1}{2}$ **2** 50%

Unit 9 Ratio

Exercise 1 (page 34)

1 **a** If 1 adult goes, $1 \times 5 = 5$ pupils can go.
 b If 2 adults go, $2 \times 5 = 10$ pupils can go.
 c If 3 adults go, $3 \times 5 = 15$ pupils can go.
 d If 9 adults go, $9 \times 5 = 45$ pupils can go.

2 **a** If 5 pupils go, $5 \div 5 = 1$ adult will be required.
 b If 10 pupils go, $10 \div 5 = 2$ adults will be required.
 c If 15 pupils go, $15 \div 5 = 3$ adults will be required
 d If 45 pupils go, $45 \div 5 = 9$ adults will be required.
3 There is 1 adult for every 5 pupils. The ratio of adults to pupils is 1 to 5 or 1 : 5.
4 There are 5 pupils for every 1 adult. The ratio of pupils to adults is 5 to 1 or 5 : 1.

Exercise 2 (page 35)

1 **a** $72 : 6 = 12 : 1$
 b 216 cars ($6 \times 3 = 18, 72 \times 3 = 216$)
2 96% (2 shares = 64%, so 1 share = 32% and 3 shares = $32 \times 3 = 96\%$)
3 The ratios are $3 : 4 : 5, 3 + 4 + 5 = 12$ shares,
 $£300 \div 12 = £25.00$
 Pat receives $3 \times £25.00 = £75.00$
 Paul receives $4 \times £25.00 = £100.00$
 Peter receives $5 \times £25.00 = £125.00$
 Check: $£75.00 + £100.00 + £125.00 = £300.00$

Unit 10 Algebra basics

Exercise 1 (page 36)

1 **a** $2c$ **b** pq **c** $\frac{3}{d}$ **d** $\frac{n}{5}$ **e** $\frac{m}{n}$ **2** Yes **3** No

Exercise 2 (page 37)

1 $10 + 2 = 12$ **2** $s + 2$
3 $8 + w$ **4** $2 \times 8 = 16$
5 $2b$ or $2 \times b$ **6** $2b - 2$ or $2 \times b - 2$

Exercise 3 (page 38)

1 $n \times n$
2 $(3 + n) \times 2$ or $2(3 + n)$
3 **a** 10 **b** 3 **c** 3
 d 2 **e** $5 \times 3 = 15$
 f $1 + 16 = 17$ ($\frac{y}{2}$ means $y \div 2$)

Exercise 4 (page 39)

1 $4h, T = 4h + 3$
2 $V = 20k, V = 20k - 75$
3 He spent $£9.99t; 9.99t + 4.54 = m$

Unit 11 How to solve equations

Exercise 1 (page 40)

1 $x = 6$ **2** $y = 8$ **3** $z = 12$

Exercise 2 (page 41)

1 $y = 9$ **2** $r = 20$ **3** $t = 9$
4 $f = 5$ **5** $x = 7$

Unit 12 Sequences

Exercise 1 (page 42)

1 The number of red squares is $p \times 2 = 2p$.
2 The number of white squares is always 4.
3 The total number of squares is $2p + 4$.

Exercise 2 (page 42)

1 4, 7, 10, 13, 16, 19, 22; The first term is 4, and each term is 3 more than the one before.
2 1, 4, 9, 16, 25, 36, 49; The first term is 1 and the first difference is 3. Each difference is 2 more than the one before. Or, you may have noticed that this is the sequence of square numbers.
3 22, 18, 14, 10, 6, 2; The first term is 22, and each number is 4 less than the one before.

ANSWERS

Exercise 3 (page 43)

1 0, 1, 2
2 3, 5, 7
3 2, 5, 10
4

Position	1	2	3	4	5	6	7	8	9	10
Term	5	7	9	11	13	15	17	19	21	23

Exercise 4 (page 43)

1 The correct sequence is 3, 7, 11, 15, 19, 23, 27, 31
2 The sequence has 8 terms.
3 6, 10, 14, 18, 22, 26, 30
4 The sequence has 7 terms.

Unit 13 Graphs

Exercise 1 (page 44)

1 E = (3, −2), F = (−4, 1)
   G = (0, −3), H = (1, 0)

Exercise 2 (page 45)

2 **a**

x	0	1	2	3	4
$y = x$	0	1	2	3	4

   b

x	0	1	2	3	4
$y = 2x$	0	2	4	6	8

   c

x	0	1	2	3	4
$y = 3x$	0	3	6	9	12

3

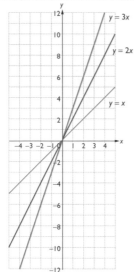

Your graphs illustrate multiplication tables.
$y = x$ is the 1 times table. You find the
y-value by multiplying the x-value by 1.
$y = 2x$ is the 2 times table. You find the
y-value by multiplying the x-value by 2.
$y = 3x$ is the 3 times table. You find the
y-value by multiplying the x-value by 3.

Exercise 3 (page 46)

1

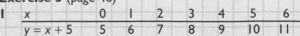

x	0	1	2	3	4	5	6
$y = x + 5$	5	6	7	8	9	10	11

2

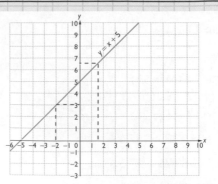

3 When $x = −2$, $y = 3$
4 When $y = 6.5$, $x = 1.5$

Exercise 4 (page 47)

1 80 kph   2 40 miles

Shape, space and measures

Unit 14 Measurement

Exercise 1 (page 50)

1 **a** 15.2 cm   **b** 2.1 cm   **c** 0.5 cm   **d** 180 cm
   e 3200 cm   **f** 45 300 cm
2 **a** 0.36 m   **b** 360 mm   **c** 0.45 m   **d** 0.0425 km
   e 0.735 km   **f** 21.462 km

Exercise 2 (page 51)

1 **a** 4000 ml   **b** 3500 ml   **c** 7200 ml   **d** 0.45 l
   e 2.163 l   **f** 0.723 l
2 **a** 2.5–3 kg   **b** 2 gallons   **c** 12.5 miles

Unit 15 Angles and lines

Exercise 1 (page 52)

1 **a** reflex   **b** obtuse   **c** acute   **d** right angle
   e reflex
2 b and c are parallel, d is perpendicular

Exercise 2 (page 53)

1 $x = \angle QPR$, $y = \angle PQR$, $u = \angle PRQ$,
   $z = \angle SRT$, $v = \angle RST$, $w = \angle STR$
2 A right-angled isosceles triangle

Exercise 3 (page 54)

1 **a** 55°   **b** 105°   **c** 105°
2 **a** $\angle BAC = 70°$ **b** $\angle ACD = 131°$
   c $\angle ABC + \angle BAC = 131°$
3 The totals are always the same.

Exercise 4 (page 55)

1 $\angle UST$ or $\angle TSU$ or $\angle RQS$ or $\angle SQR$
2 **a** $\angle TUS$ **b** $\angle VWU$ 3 $\angle QXS$ or $\angle SXQ$
4 $\angle WUV$ or $\angle VUW$ 5 SU   6 RQ
7 **a** $\angle SUT$ or $\angle TUS$
   b $\angle WUV$ or $\angle VUW$
8 $\angle RST$ or $\angle TSR$, $\angle TSU$ or $\angle UST$, $\angle USX$ or $\angle XSU$,
   $\angle XSQ$ or $\angle QSX$, $\angle QSR$ or $\angle RSQ$

Unit 16 Polygons

Exercise 1 (page 56)

Number of sides	Number of triangles
4	2
5	3
6	4
7	5
8	6
9	7
10	8

The number of sides is always 2 more than the number of triangles.

The formula is $T = S - 2$ or $S - 2 = T$

Exercise 2 (page 57)

1 540°   2 1080°   3 900°

4 3240°

Unit 17 Constructions

Exercise 1 (page 58)

$a = 60°$ $b = 45°$ $c = 70°$

$d = 110°$ $e = 160°$

Exercise 2 (page 59)

1

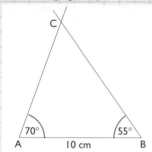

2, 3 AC = AB = 10 cm

4 The triangle is isosceles.

Unit 18 Two-dimensional shapes

Exercise 1 (page 60)

1 135° The angles round a point add up to 360° and the angles at each vertex of the square are 90°.

2 360° − 90° = 270°, 270° ÷ 2 = 135°

3 120° (360° ÷ 3 = 120°)

4 They all will except pentagons.

Exercise 2 (page 61)

1 E   2 D   3 F   4 B

5 A   6 C

Unit 19 Area and perimeter

Exercise 1 (page 62)

1 46 cm   2 100 cm or 1 m   3 24 cm

Exercise 2 (page 63)

1 68 cm²

2 The outside area is 20 × 30 = 600 cm²

The inside area is (20 − 2) × (30 − 2)

   = 18 × 28 = 504 cm²

600 − 504 = 96 cm²

3 24 cm²

Unit 20 Views

Exercise 1 (page 64)

1 40 cubes

2 10 cm²

3 8 cm²

4

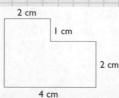

Exercise 2 (page 65)

a   side elevation

b   front elevation

c   plan

Unit 21 Transformations

Exercise 1 (page 66)

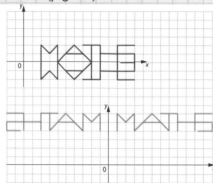

Exercise 2 (page 67)

1 K, M, T, U, V, W, Y   2 None

3 O, X

4 J, L, N, P, Q, R, S, Z

Exercise 3 (page 67)

1 3 units right and 4 units down.

2 4 units left and 6 units up

Exercise 4 (page 68)

1, 2

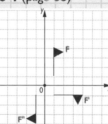

3 180°

4 It does not matter which way you go. 180° is halfway round the centre of rotation.

Exercise 5 (page 69)

1 a Shape S maps to S′ by a reflection in the y-axis.

   b Shape S′ maps to S″ by a rotation of 90° anticlockwise centred at O.

   c Shape S″ maps to S′ by a by a rotation of 90° clockwise centred at O.

   d Shape S′ maps to S by a reflection in the y-axis.

2 a A translation of 9 units to the left, and 2 down.

   b A reflection in the x-axis.

   c A reflection in the x-axis.

   d A translation of 9 units to the right and 2 up.

3 No. Experiment to see the difference.

Handling data

Unit 22 Averages and range

Exercise 1 (page 72)

1 a mode 6   b mean 7   c median 6

2 a mode 1.5   b mean 2.65

   c median 2.25

Exercise 2 (page 73)

1 a mean = 9   b median = 8

   c mode = 8   d 15 − 4 = 11

ANSWERS

Unit 23 Samples and surveys
Exercise I (page 74)
I   **a**   95%   **b**   25%   **c**   10%   **d**   20%
2

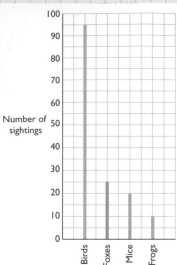

Exercise 2 (page 75)
I   **a**   Thursday   **b**   Monday and Friday
   c   20 packets   **d**   Wednesday
2   pink 180°, blue 90°, yellow 18°, green 54°, other 18°

Unit 24 Probability

Exercise I (page 76)
I   Likely
2   Equally likely
3   Impossible. (It is possible, though that Josh will not take a red marble, so both could score zero for red.)
4   Jake   5   0.5

Exercise 2 (page 77)
I   **a** $\frac{4}{5}$ **b**   0.35   **c**   0.7   **d**   100%   **e** $\frac{5}{8}$

2   **a**   0.375   **b**   38%
3   **a**   HH, HT, TH, TT
   b $\frac{1}{4}$ **c** $\frac{3}{4}$ **d** $\frac{1}{2}$

Exercise 3 (page 77)
I   0.125   2   0.25
3   0.64 (The quickest way is to start by subtracting the number of students choosing football from the total number of students.

Answers to specimen tests

Test Paper I

Mental arithmetic test

I 10 009	10 kite	18 $\frac{2}{5}$
2 626	II 30	19 40°
3 56	12 10	20 6.35 metres
4 6 500 000	13 12 cm²	21 $7\frac{1}{2}$ or 7.5
5 24 cm	14 13	22 $n + 6$
6 $\frac{12}{20} = \frac{3}{5}$ or 0.6	15 75%	23 £6.00
7 19	16 8	24 0.064
8 $3\frac{1}{8}$	17 4	25 10
9 11 ($11^2 = 121, 12^2 = 144.$ 121 is closer to 131 than 144 is.)		

Test paper 2
I   **a**   To change centimetres to metres, divide by 100.
   b   To change centimetres to millimetres, multiply by 10.
   c   To change tonnes to kilograms, multiply by 1000.
   d   To change grams to kilograms, divide by 1000.
2   **a** 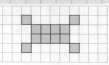

   b $2 \times 15 + 4 = 34$ squares
3   **a**   3 : 2 : 1
   b $3 + 2 + 1 = 6, 18 \div 6 = 3, 3 \times 3 = 9$ litres red, $2 \times 3 = 6$ litres green, $1 \times 3 = 3$ litres blue
   c   She only has half the amount of blue which she needs, so she can only make 9 litres of the mixture.
   d   She is short of half of the amount she needs.
4

Kite

5

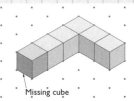

Missing cube

6   **a**   25   **b**   square numbers
7   **a** $6 \times 20 = 120$
   b   If the range of the scores is eight, one number must be four above the mean, and one number must be four below, so the missing numbers are 16 and 24.
8   **a**   square
   b   He is wrong because there are more cards left with squares than there are with stars.
   c   She is wrong because there are more cards left unpicked with squares than there are with stars.
9   10% $(50 + 20 + 17 + 3 = 90, 100\% - 90\% = 10\%)$
10   **a**   −2°   **b**   5°
11   **a**   Assume a coach can carry 50 people, $400 \div 50 = 8$
   b $415 \div 56 = 7.41$ (2 d.p.) so 8 coaches are needed.
12   **a** $a = 180° - 110° = 70°$
   b $b = 180° - (60° + a) = 50°$
   c $c = 180° - (110° + 40°) = 30°$

13 Angle *a* and angle *e* are acute angles.
Angle *b* and angle *c* are obtuse angles.
Angle *d* and angle *f* are reflex angles.

14 a 9310

   b 9310, 9130, 3910, 3190, 1390, 1930

15

Burgers	Chips
cheeseburger	small
cheeseburger	large
beefburger	small
beefburger	large
veggieburger	small
veggieburger	large

16 a 6 cm   **b** 6 cm × 4 = 24 cm

   c 20 (4 along the width and 5 along the length, 4 × 5 = 20)

Test paper 3

1 a 16 ÷ 2 + 23 = 31

   b i (5 + 7) × 2 = 24

     ii (20 − 5) ÷ (2 + 3) = 3

   c Without brackets, 5 + 7 × 2 = 19 and 20 − 5 ÷ 2 + 3 = 20.5 or $20\frac{1}{2}$

2 They are all true.

3 a 19.2   **b** 5.95

4 a 13   **b** 6

5 a 68.16   **b** 2408.57   **c** 839.40

6 a

   b 70° + 35° = 105°
180° − 105° = 75°

7 a

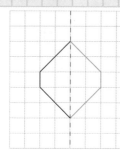

   b hexagon   **c** 1 cm²   **d** 12 cm²

8

```
A                                    B
|                                    |
0                0.5                 1
```

9 a 0.7 km   **b** 0.3 km

   c 10 minutes   **d** 5 minutes

   e 7.5 minutes   **f** 12.5 minutes

   g 0.7 km × 2 = 1.4 km

10 a £187.50   **b** £6.25   **c** £6.00

11 a £15.50   **b** £9.30   **c** £77.50

12 a 54%

   b 90° (There are 360° in a complete turn. 25% of 360° = $\frac{1}{4}$ of 360°)

13 28 students (7 : 3 = ? : 12, 3 × 4 = 12, 7 × 4 = 28)

14

		Spinner A					
		1	2	3	4	5	6
Spinner B	1	2	3	4	5	6	7
	3	4	5	6	7	8	9
	5	6	7	8	9	10	11

Unlikely, because more outcomes are 7 or less than are more than 7.

15 a

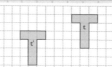

   b 6 units right and 2 units up

JARGON BUSTER

angle	amount or turn where two (or more) lines meet
area	the flat space occupied by a plane shape, or inside it
axis of symmetry	mirror line
axis (plural **axes**)	the vertical or horizontal line on a graph; the line that divides a symmetrical shape into two exact mirror images
biased	event which is more likely to give one outcome than another
commutative	an operation where the order does not matter (Multiplication is commutative because $3 \times 2 = 2 \times 3$.)
congruent	identical
consecutive	following without a gap
consecutive numbers	numbers that follow on in order, e.g. 1, 2, 3, …
cube	a 3D solid with square faces
cuboid	a 3D solid with rectangular faces
decagon	a ten-sided polygon
digit	individual numeral in a number: 6 has one digit, 20 has two digits, as does 3.4
dividend	a number or quantity to be divided (In the example $6 \div 2$, six is the dividend.)
divisor	the number that is divided by (In the example $6 \div 2$, two is the divisor.)
edge	where two faces of a solid meet
equidistant	at the same distance
equilateral	equal sided
evaluate	find the value
expression	two or more terms in a formula, e.g. $4n + 2$
exterior angle	the angle formed at a vertex (corner) outside a polygon if one side is extended
factor	a number that divides into another number or quantity exactly, e.g. 4 is a factor of 8

frequency	the number of times an event happens
frequency diagram	a diagram to show the frequency of an event, e.g. a bar chart
front elevation	the view of an object from the front
hexagon	a six-sided polygon
horizontal axis	the axis in a graph that goes across, usually the x-axis (The **horizon** is horizontal.)
integer	whole number
interior angle	the angle inside the vertex (corner) of a polygon
intersect	cross (Lines that cross each other are **intersecting lines**.)
intersection	the point where two lines cross
inverse process	a process that 'undoes' the previous process (Addition and subtraction are inverse processes, and multiplication and division are inverse processes.)
isosceles triangle	a triangle with two sides the same and two angles the same
mean	the sum of all the values in a set of data, divided by the number of values in the set
median	the middle value of a set of data arranged in order from left to right, smallest to largest
modal group	the range of values that occurs most often (has the highest frequency) in a set of grouped data, e.g. ages 5–9
mode	the most common value in a given set (the value with the highest frequency)
multiple	a number with two or more factors, a number formed by multiplying two other numbers, e.g. 12 is a multiple of 3, 20 is a multiple of 10
net	a hollow 3D shape opened up and laid flat

numeral   single figure in a number, like a letter in a word

octagon   an eight-sided polygon

outcome   the result of an event in probability (Throwing a penny has two possible outcomes, head or tail.)

parallel   two (or more) lines that are always equidistant from each other (Spelling hint: The two letter ls in the word 'parallel' are parallel lines.)

parallelogram   a four-sided shape with one pair of opposite sides equal and parallel (In fact, both pairs are equal and parallel, but the proof will come in later years.)

pentagon   a five-sided polygon

perimeter   the distance all round a shape

perpendicular   meeting or intersecting at right angles (90°)

plan view   a view of an object looking down from above

polygon   a two-dimensional (2D), straight-sided shape with three or more sides

probability scale   a measure of probability, like a number line, from 0 to 1

product   the result of multiplying two numbers together

quadrant   a quarter of a graph grid (The x- and y-axes divide a graph into four quadrants.)

quadrilateral   a four-sided polygon

quotient   the result of dividing a number or amount by another number (In $6 \div 2 = 3$, the quotient is 3.)

random   by chance (A random sample is one in which all members of the group have equal chances of being chosen.)

range   the largest value minus the smallest value in a set of data

rhombus   a quadrilateral with all sides equal and opposite sides parallel (the diagonals cross at right angles.) It resembles a diamond.

sample   group or people taken as being typical, to take part in a survey

scalene triangle   triangle in which each side is a different length and all angles are different

sequence of numbers   a list of numbers that form a pattern according to a given rule

side elevation   the view of an object from the side

simplify   collect together all the same variables in an expression or equation, e.g. $1 + 2t + 1 + 3t + 2 = 5t + 4$

sum   the total of two or more numbers added together

survey   research, find out people's opinions by asking questions

term   a number in a sequence (The first number is the first term, the next is the second term, and so on.)

trapezium   a quadrilateral with one pair of sides parallel but unequal

unbiased   an event in which all outcomes have an equal chance of occurring

variable   numbers that do not necessarily have a fixed value, but vary, usually represented by letters in algebra

vertex   corner (The plural is **vertices**.)

vertical   upright

vertical axis   the axis in a graph that goes up and down the page, at right angles to the horizontal axis, and usually called the y-axis

vertices   corners, plural of **vertex**

INDEX